# SMU REFLECTIONS

Edited by

Bonnie Brunk Hillerbrand

and Donna Booth Salacuse

# SMU REFLECTIONS

Photography Edited by

Elizabeth Perkins Prothro

Southern Methodist

University Press

1986

Composed by Princeton University Press,
Princeton, New Jersey

Printed and Bound by Dai Nippon, Ltd.,
Tokyo, Japan

Designed by Laury A. Egan

The paper in this book meets the standards for
permanence and durability established by the
Committee on Production Guidelines for Book
Longevity of the Council on Library Resources.

Library of Congress
Cataloguing-in-Publication Data
SMU reflections.
Includes index.
    1. Southern Methodist University—
Description—Views.   2. Southern Methodist
University—History.   I. Hillerbrand, Bonnie
Brunk.   II. Salacuse, Donna Booth.   III. Prothro,
Elizabeth Perkins.
LD5101.S36533S58 1986   378.764'2812  86-
11809
ISBN 0-87074-219-1

To all who have been a part of Southern Methodist University

The names of those who laid the foundations are unknown to the students of today, but I was a part of the University's life when men vied with one another for recognition as founders of the University. In view of what the University has become, there is really honor enough for all of those who belong to its first days, even if their names are no longer remembered . . . Today and tomorrow at SMU must build on the yesterdays.

IVAN LEE HOLT

PHOTOGRAPHY BY

ELIZABETH PERKINS PROTHRO

JANET SAVILLE COLEMAN        NAN COULTER        PAUL S. TALLEY

# CONTENTS

# Acknowledgments

This book would not have been possible without access to a wide variety of materials located in various departments and libraries of the University. We acknowledge the special assistance of Lee Milazzo, Virginia Bols, and Peter Bickel of the SMU Archives; Gerald McGee, Pat Porter, and David Schulz of University Relations; Dorothy Haralson, Secretary of the University; Robert Oram of University Libraries; Travis Jordan of Media Services; the Law School; Dedman College; and the offices of Alumni Relations, Meadows Public Relations, and Sports Information.

Jim Brooks, Ron Davis, and Bill and Pat Stallcup shared their resources and directed us to University treasures. Numerous volunteers of the SMU Woman's Club aided in research, especially Lorene Prewitt. The SMU Woman's Club Oral History Group contributed through their interviews, as did interviewees who permitted the use of quotations from their transcripts and others who contributed through copyrighted material.

Janet Coleman, Nan Coulter, and Paul Talley responded with enthusiasm to our project and offered their experience as well as their photography. Mary Scofield helped judge slides from the artistic standpoint. The office of Charles W. Culwell arranged for a photographic visit to Peruna. Our ability to offer a book with accurate citations is in large part due to the conscientious research of Jeni Umble. Bonnie Harris, Pamela Skillman, and Patty Smith gave typing assistance. Johnnie Marie Grimes and Judy Mohraz read the manuscript and offered valuable suggestions.

Our husbands and families showed patience and offered encouragement, as did the 75th Anniversary Committee of the University and the Editorial Board and staff of the SMU Press.

We are truly indebted to them all for their generous and thoughtful sharing in a task that was for us—and them—a labor of love for SMU.

B.B.H.

E.P.P.

D.B.S.

# INTRODUCTION

A university campus is more than buildings and landscapes; it is also memories and traditions. Since its founding in 1911, Southern Methodist University has transformed a portion of the harsh Texas prairie north of Dallas into a harmonious and inviting environment, a complex of buildings and walkways, libraries and classrooms, that remains indelibly and affectionately etched into the memories of its nearly 70,000 alumni and alumnae. For them, SMU is the "Hilltop," and its architecture is given meaning by their own experiences and recollections.

The history of SMU is both the story of the growth of a university campus and the story of its students, faculty, and staff. This book seeks to present the SMU campus in its historical context. Its goal is to portray the University's history through the recollections of those who lived it. The quotations reflect the years 1911 through the 1980s and take the reader from the origins of the campus to its contemporary appearance. Thus, *SMU Reflections* does reflect the past and present through words as well as through photographs.

In most instances a book is written and photographs are used to illustrate the text. Here we have used a chronological and thematical framework for the contemporary color photographs based on the order in which buildings were begun or departments were established. We then sought oral and written material to "illustrate" the photographs, the selection of photographs governed by the focus of the book. We have used special care to choose textual material that reflects the themes and mood of a given era. The quotations are of necessity shortened and are taken from informative contexts that were oftentimes so interesting that we would have enjoyed following the material rather than maintaining the focus we had determined for the book.

The Hilltop in Dallas attracted students to its first classes from far and wide, but far and wide in those days meant from Shreveport to Waxahachie. The student body in the early years included the nineteen year old who followed his friend from junior college to Dallas and later became editor of a national magazine. Then there was the young woman who took the streetcar daily from Oak Cliff, as did many SMU students. She loved literature and went on to become head of the theatre department of her alma mater. A young

# · FRED · A · JONES · BUILDING · COMPANY ·

HOUSTON                    DALLAS                    BIRMINGHAM

THE · FRED · A · JONES · CO ·
ENGINEERS
HOUSTON · TEXAS ·
DALLAS · TEXAS ·

· LOUIS · ROBERT · BARRAS ·
VICE · PRESIDENT AND · GENERAL · MANAGER

· PRAETORIAN · BUILDING · DALLAS · TEXAS ·  May 27, 1912.


Shepley, Rutan & Coolidge, Archts.,
Southern Methodist University,
Commerce St.,
Dallas, Texas.

Gentlemen:

We hereby propose to furnish all the labor and
materials required in the construction of the Dallas Hall
building in strict accordance with your drawings and speci-
fications for the sum of *Two hundred twelve*
*thousand, nine hundred two* ($212,902.00/100) Dollars.

Add the sum of *Eleven hundred*
($1100.00) _____ Dollars
if face brick is laid in Flemish Bond.

We beg further to submit the following unit prices
for the additions to the work:

Additional earth excavation *0.65 (Cents)* per cubic yard.
Additional concrete foundation work *$7 50/100*

per cubic yard.

In all buildings, as well as this one, there are
numerous changes which could be made to materially reduce
the cost of same, and should it be your desire, we would be
pleased to submit you revised quotations taking into considera-
tion any changes that you might care to consider.

Should we be awarded this contract, we would agree
to start work immediately and to finish the completion of the
building within eleven (11) months from date of delivery of
site and complete drawings.

Yours very truly,

Fred A. Jones Building Company.

By *Carl Symonds*
Houston Manager.

CS/KL.

xii

(Above) Dallas Hall under construction. The first building on SMU's campus was planned to be "a magnificent fireproof structure and of such architectural beauty as to be worthy of the crowning feature of the campus." (Right) Hoisting into place one of the capitals that crown the six Corinthian columns of the portico of Dallas Hall.

man came a great distance from Louisiana because he wanted to become a preacher but upon reaching SMU was told he would have to obtain a degree before entering theology school; he later became a Methodist Bishop. Another student was "colored red and blue" for the rest of his life after seeing SMU beat Texas at Austin in 1926. He later became SMU's longest-tenured President, receiving the Alexander Meiklejohn Award "for significant action in support of academic freedom."

As newcomers to SMU and Dallas several years ago, we were often startled by the immediacy of the past. Conversational references to "Father having settled this land" or "Grandmother having come in a covered wagon" made storybook themes very real. Our new acquaintances spoke of SMU's first faculty as their friends or professors. The notion that history was within touching distance led us to reach for it before its participants passed on.

The SMU Woman's Club became a source of talent and primary history in our quest. In 1982, faculty wives and women faculty founded an oral history interest group within the club. A generous grant from President L. Donald Shields provided equipment and transcription funds, while faculty and staff helped in training the volunteer interviewers. After recording equipment was purchased and a release form developed, the group drew up a list of potential interviewees by relying on personal contacts and suggestions from various University departments. Volunteers conducted the interviews, and many interviewees came from the early classes at the University.

All interviewees were contacted through a letter which described the project and requested an interview. The responses were varied. Some asked to be interviewed immediately; others had to be persuaded; and a few refused. Interviews during the first three years of the project have produced a wealth of information.

The excerpts from interviews used in this book have been edited for clarity and continuity. Although the material chosen had been previously released, as a matter of courtesy we advised the interviewees of our intent to publish their edited words. Faced with publication, interviewees sometimes returned to us "improved" versions—a factor which complicated parts of the project, because we strove to maintain the conversational manner rather than a written style. At times we would have preferred the original. It has also been necessary to keep the style of the quotations (some from published and others from unpublished sources) somewhat consistent with the letters, speeches, and articles from which they were excerpted. In all instances, we have committed ourselves to the highest attainable integrity regarding the context of the quotations.

The work of the oral history project is ongoing. Its importance cannot be stressed enough. The role of our generation is to record faithfully the reminiscences of the founders and the builders of SMU so that those who follow us will understand and value their heritage.

We have also drawn on other historical sources. As we undertook this project, we dis-

Coeds pose in front of the streetcar, the "Dinkey," the link between the campus and downtown Dallas in 1917.

1947
SMU...19
TCU...19

Walker outdistances frogs as he rambles 76 yards for score. *Laughead*

Football would continue to excite SMU students: Doak Walker and teammates at the TCU game in 1947.

covered that the University Archives contained taped interviews of oral history which had been conducted by University Archivist Lee Milazzo. Funds from the oral history project allowed some of these important interviews to be transcribed. In order to fill gaps where no oral history resources existed, we have borrowed from the files of the SMU Archives, Bridwell Library, Fondren Library, and the SMU Law School, as well as from the student newspaper, *The Daily Campus*, the yearbook, *The Rotunda*, and the alumni magazine, *The Mustang*, in some instances. We have used letters and speeches from private collections. We are especially indebted to the work of Herbert Gambrell, formerly Chairman of the History Department, who, following his retirement in 1964, collected much material through extensive letter writing laced with his own memories, which in turn led others to recall the past.

Early on, we realized that we shared James F. White's appreciation of the architecture of the SMU campus, so ably illustrated in his 1966 booklet, *Architecture at SMU: 50 Years and Buildings*. We made early morning treks with the light of the sun just coming up, late afternoon walks in the summer heat, and intermittent visits to special celebrations of the academic world such as Convocation, Homecoming, athletic and artistic events, and Commencement. All of these visits sensitized and trained our eyes to see beautiful details that weren't evident to us before. We discovered the rhythm and order of founding President Robert S. Hyer's grand design for the campus. We found that the history of the University could be told through the chronology of its buildings.

We have made no attempt to cover in detail or historical perspective the material handled so well by James F. White's *Architecture at SMU*, Mary Martha Hosford Thomas's *Southern Methodist University: Founding and Early Years*, Johnnie Marie Grimes's *Willis M. Tate: Views and Interviews*, and Ray Hyer Brown's *Robert Stewart Hyer, The Man I Knew*.* We have cited from each where necessary for continuity.

The idea for this book coincided with plans for the celebration of the seventy-fifth anniversary of SMU's founding. What better way to commemorate seventy-five years of history than with an album of photographs! Elizabeth Perkins Prothro, alumna, Trustee, and committed supporter of the University through the years, accepted the challenge of photographing the campus and serving as Photography Editor. She has taken hundreds of photographs and has been responsible for the direction of cooperating photographers. She has coordinated the search through a number of departmental and personal collections, making the final selection from close to two thousand photographs. The extensive photographic knowledge she has brought to the project and her intimate experience with SMU's past and present have made her contribution invaluable.

A project such as this is never complete; it is only called to an end by the publisher's deadline. It leaves unused hundreds of fine photographs, countless informative tapes and

* The first three were published in 1966, 1974, and 1978, respectively, by the SMU Press and are still in print. Mrs. Brown's book was published by the Anson Jones Press in 1957.

interviews, and many rich private resources not yet reviewed. Any reader knowledgable about SMU will notice many stellar names missing from our text. We were unable to include every building, donor, and department, much as we would have liked, because of constraints of time and space. We want to assure all those who have given interviews and suggested directions for study, and all those who have given gifts to establish buildings and to purchase landscaping, books, and equipment—as well as their friends and families—that this book and our lives, as well as the life of the school and the community, have been immeasurably enriched by their contributions. We have a very real concern and hope that the treasures hidden in the files and closets of individual departments as well as those in private collections will be assembled in a central location or catalogued by a central coordinator, so that the history of this community might be preserved.

In his interview, Professor Marshall Terry aptly summarizes and echoes our concern: "I suddenly realized the truth of how little memory an institution has . . . . New people hardly know the things that I go around remembering . . . . We need a shared sense of ourselves."

The chronology of the major buildings and facilities to be found at the end of this book summarizes the growth of the University and the names of educators, administrators, trustees, and donors who have played an essential part in the history of SMU. In one sense, it is an honor roll of those who have contributed to the growth of this great institution. But as an honor roll, it is incomplete, for there are many builders for whom no structure is named.

We have intended *SMU Reflections*—really a labor of love—to be more than a coffee-table book. We have striven for accuracy in the Index of Interviewees and Sources, and we feel confident that these citations will enable others to follow any historical interest they might have.

Taped interviews formed the core of the book. We include here an excerpt longer than those used in the text in order to illustrate the techniques used and to suggest the mood and rhythm of the personal interaction. The interview, which spans the earliest years to the present, was made in January 1986 by Professor Judy Mohraz, a member of the SMU Woman's Club Oral History Group, with Eva B Slater, a founding member and a great inspiration to that group. Mrs. Slater was a freshman at SMU in 1922 and majored in French. She began a master of arts program in 1926 and left to teach but returned in 1928. She married Eugene Slater in November 1931 and left Dallas, to return in 1976. At that time, Bishop Slater became Bishop in Residence at the Perkins School of Theology until his retirement in 1980.

MOHRAZ: I wonder if you would begin with being a freshman at SMU and the sharpest, most memorable visions and recollections you have of what it was like to be a freshman in 1922.

SLATER: I came out on a bright spring afternoon to Dallas Hall to register to come to SMU. There was Johnson grass, as everybody knows, but the gaillardias (Indian blankets) were in bloom all over and it was a beautiful campus. Dallas Hall, if you can imagine how it would look all by itself on the hill in 1922, was the only building anywhere around. Everything took place in Dallas Hall. As a freshman I had English, math, French, Spanish, and chemistry—with two three-hour labs each week—all in Dallas Hall. I remember that in the basement there was the Co-op, also the store, the post office, work rooms for the library, and a few tiny offices for various professors. There were only fifteen faculty members when SMU opened; this number increased to about sixty-five in the twenties. I think you would call it ingrown, because many of the teachers had graduated from SMU and had a year of graduate work here and were preparing to go on to graduate school. There were two men who had been Rhodes scholars. I had physics from Dr. Hyer when I was a senior. He acted like every student was a part of his family. He would stop us on the campus and visit. He would stop us after class and be sure we had understood what was being done. Wherever he would meet us there was always a moment of friendly conversation. He was a sparkling conversationalist and interested in everything the students were interested in.

MOHRAZ: As a student, what were your perceptions of the controversy in 1923 to 1925 about Professor Workman?

SLATER: Some of the students, I am sure, were sympathetic with the more fundamental interpretation of the Scripture, but some of us were more interested in the way Dr. Workman presented it. He taught what was commonly accepted as the liberal viewpoint. He was very creative and he challenged us, if we didn't like what was said, to find something else, but to be sure we had a reason for accepting it.

MOHRAZ: How did students perceive the women faculty?

SLATER: I think that Miss Whitsett in Chemistry was definitely taken as a serious scholar. She was an excellent teacher. For my first-year English teacher, Marie Dora Hempke, every sentence had to be complete, every bit of punctuation had to be exact. Miss Amann was a woman of great ability, determination, and strong will. She was sent to visit libraries in established universities in this country although there was no money to buy books. She gave me a job when I was a freshman and I stayed in the library all the time I was a student. I started at thirty-five cents an hour, and that was exactly enough to pay my tuition.

Miss Amann gave the Mustangs their name. She remarked one day, "Why out there on the football field, it just looks like a bunch of mustangs!" Of course, if you've lived in Texas very long, you know that mustangs are wild ponies in the hill country.

MOHRAZ: You were here for the fire of 1926?

SLATER: Oh, yes. The big fire of 1926 engulfed three dormitories. They were called North Hall, South Hall, and Rankin Hall. They were close to Airline Road. They made a sort

*S. M. U.'s Disastrous Fire—The Three
Dormitories Destroyed in Less
Than One Hour*

The great fire of 1926. A page from the *Rotunda* of that year.

of hollow three-sided square. I don't know what caused the fire, but I remember distinctly that University Park had a brand-new fire engine, about a ten-thousand dollar fire engine, and it answered the call at once. It rolled right up in that hollow space between the dormitories and began to pour water on the fire. Suddenly, one of the firemen decided he had better move the fire engine because the fire was getting closer. It couldn't be moved because it was mired in the black mud, and they had to leave it there, where it burned. Everything on the campus just automatically shut down and everybody went to see the fire. We lost three dormitories and a fire engine on one afternoon in February.

MOHRAZ: Tell me about the files in the dome.

SLATER: Well, one of the places that one goes when he's interested in periodicals is into the back files, and we didn't have a lot of room for back files in the area of Dallas Hall that was given over to the periodical division. We had a big reading room but the files were all in that little office in the little curved part of the west end of the basement, and many, many, many of the files, old magazines, and newspapers that were being kept by the library were housed in the dome of Dallas Hall. As I remember, the back files were just stacked open there; they were not sacked up or put in boxes but there they were, tied in bundles. A year of this and a year of that until somebody needed it. I'm so glad we now have Fondren Library to house the files.

MOHRAZ: Also, what about the golf course? I didn't know we had a golf course.

SLATER: Well, there was so much land around there, all covered with Johnson grass, south of Dallas Hall and over where the Ownby oval is now. Before that there was just nothing on that part of the campus, and there were nine crude golf holes there. And sometimes on a spring day you would see maybe half a dozen ambitious golfers out there with their clubs, or maybe just one club, playing . . . . I think I played that course maybe twice or three times when I was in SMU.

MOHRAZ: When McFarlin Auditorium was built, that must have been a major event since it was such an impressive structure.

SLATER: It *was* a major event. One of the things that President Selecman wanted at that time was a place where all the students could come at one time. Thirty-four hundred people could sit in McFarlin, plus two hundred on the stage. My class was the first class to graduate from McFarlin!

MOHRAZ: Do you remember Dr. Umphrey Lee?

SLATER: Oh my yes. I remember him vividly. He was a minister at Highland Park Methodist Church and that's where we went. He was one of the most erudite men I have ever met. Dr. Lee was polished and had a very keen sense of humor. He had a way of telling his seminary students, "You might as well get through [preaching] in twenty minutes because that's about as much as you have to say, and besides, people are beginning to get hungry." Highland Park Methodist Church was a little brown frame

(Above) Students promenade Bishop Boulevard toward Dallas Hall, with parasols to keep the hot sun off the ladies' faces. (Below) Looking from Hillcrest Avenue to Dallas Hall at University Boulevard. The markers were a gift from the Class of 1922.

building on the corner of Mockingbird and Hillcrest with a boardwalk up from the streetcar line. Dr. Lee was the minister there for many years and greatly beloved.

MOHRAZ: SMU's decision to desegregate began in the Perkins School, didn't it?

SLATER: There were four black students who first came to SMU in the fifties. . . .They have had places of leadership in the church since their graduation.

MOHRAZ: You have seen three generations of SMU. What makes SMU distinctive in your mind?

SLATER: I think that it has grown and increased in academic achievement and that we still have goals to meet and plans to perfect. I can't help but think my degree is worth more now than it was the day I got it. I still don't speak French, but I think SMU is a fine school.

Aerial photo of SMU campus in 1922. Note the three men's dormitories at right: North Hall, South Hall, and Rankin Hall.

# DALLAS HALL

*Dedicated to Dr. R. S. Hyer*

### I

A ghost-dome half-seen in the morning mist it stands
As when they saw it like a phantom rise—a dream—
    Those who had eyes to see.

### II

It stood before them as they cleared the brambled plain,
Dug deep the black mud, walked through deep-plowed fields in rain
To dedicate the cornerstone; they gazed at it
Through eyes half-dimmed with tears, and hopes when hope was vain—
    Those who had eyes to see.

### III

A dream of art, a dream of beauty, and a goal
Of inspiration, not efficiency alone
They saw through half-enshrouding mists, and labored on—
    Those who had eyes to see.

### IV

The mist rises! the dream lives! the sun reveals the dome
That towers over rolling plain; and columns sheer,
Pilasters tall, and light through stately porticos
(The fruits mature of tears dropped in the blackland loam)
Stands as a monument, a shrine of truth, and praise
    Those who had eyes to see.

AUBREY BURNS

# SMU REFLECTIONS

One day in 1911 a group of church and local dignitaries visited some vacant land on the northern outskirts of Dallas. The site they inspected consisted of about a quarter-section of land . . . near the intersection of present Athens Street and Daniels Avenue . . . to near Hillcrest Road and Potomac Street. Diagonally transversing the slope was a small ravine then leading from near the intersection of present Dyer Street and Airline Road to Potomac and Hillcrest . . . . A few trees were scattered about on the banks of the ravine and here and there throughout the surrounding open countryside. This was the future home of Southern Methodist University.

JAMES F. WHITE

Father took Mother and me out over the narrow dirt road through fields of waving grain. . . . On a small incline he stopped the car and said, "This is where Dallas Hall will stand." My mother burst into tears saying, "You have lost your mind, you can't build a university in the middle of this prairie." On the way home no one spoke a word.

MARGARET HYER THOMAS

President Hyer accepted the difficult challenge. . . . He wanted "one great building . . . of such architectural beauty as to be the crowning feature of the campus." . . . No detail was too small for Dr. Hyer's attention, from selecting the dignified neo-Georgian architectural style . . . to picking the school's colors (red from Harvard, blue from Yale), to choosing the University's motto "Veritas Liberabit Vos"—The Truth Shall Make You Free.

LEE MILAZZO

Father had seen Thomas Jefferson's University of Virginia and the classic neo-Georgian buildings in England—and nothing less would do but a building with a bronze dome and fluted Corinthian columns. He didn't have small ideas for this University.

And so the plans went forward and Dallas Hall was begun. With no roads to the building site it was necessary to build a spur railroad line to bring in the materials. The tracks were from the Katy line near Mockingbird Lane to about where Fondren Library now stands. Those columns of Indiana limestone had to be shipped on flatcars to Soumethun, Texas. Soumethun is an acronym for Southern Methodist University.

MARGARET HYER THOMAS

Dallas Hall, lone and imposing, sat on top of the hill, surrounded by acres and acres of Indian blankets, black-eyed Susans, and Johnson grass. Beyond its boundaries were farms, from which at June harvest came myriads of almost microscopic insects that kept us busy brushing off our faces, hands, and books, and shaking out our hair. . . . The only other buildings to break the prairie view were the Woman's Building and three temporary affairs, which housed the boys, far removed from the woman's dormitory.

GOLDIE CAPERS SMITH

The *Dallas Morning News* of June 15, 1915, carried a small drawing of the steps of Dallas Hall with me perched on the steps. The caption under the drawing read, "First student to enroll at SMU was Miss Flora Lowrey of Hillsboro, Texas, who presented her credits to Frank Reedy, Bursar."

FLORA LOWREY

About the first week of August 1915, I made my initial visit to the campus. There was a large stack of several tons of baled hay on the campus about where McFarlin Auditorium now stands. Hillcrest Avenue was a graveled country road and quite dusty. It ended at the north edge of the campus. There were no sidewalks, but I never questioned all of this, for when I walked into Dallas Hall and looked up into the rotunda, I said, "This is where I want to come to school."

HEMPHILL HOSFORD

Some folks said it couldn't be done, others said it wouldn't be done, but there were those who said it would and could and should be done. And they did it. Southern Methodist University is a reality. It has seen the first homesick freshmen arrive, go through the grind; it has seen mid-terms and finals; it has seen precedents established. It will be the privilege of posterity to hang over the railing of the rotunda, but we did it first! Posterity can never see the first tree planted, the first plough uprooting the waving Johnson grass, the first issue of the *Dinkey*, and all the other things that have gone to make this first year memorable.

ROTUNDA, 1916

People all over Texas had subscribed to the building fund for Southern Methodist University, but only Dallas money went into the building of Dallas Hall. Many contributors signed promises to pay a certain amount over a period of five years. After the war started in Europe, many of these people could not make their promised payments. A great many of them were cotton farmers or men in allied business. At the beginning of the war cotton prices dropped to three cents a pound with a big crop on hand. All sorts of plans and schemes were started to improve the market. There was a slogan, "Buy a bale of Cotton," and on the front porch of many a house there was a bale that had been purchased in answer to that plea.

Father and Mr. Reedy worked out a plan to remedy this lack of payment of money promised to the University. The University promised to take cotton from farmers who could not make this year's payment, giving them credit at the rate of ten cents a pound. Many people took advantage of this offer. (This was before school opened.) Dallas Hall was almost completed, and the basement became a cotton warehouse. I do not know just how long the cotton stayed there, but it was sold just before school opened, and while the University did not make any profit from the transaction, it did not lose any money by this plan.

RAY HYER BROWN

It may be hard for the student today to realize, but during my tenure in the University, . . . chapel attendance was compulsory.

On the third floor of Dallas Hall the west wing was all one room, an auditorium with a platform, at each end of which was a small waiting-room for speakers and with the remainder of the long room filled with rows of seats for students.

At the sound of the ten o'clock bell we filed upstairs to chapel and took our assigned seats, freshmen in front, sophomores, juniors, and seniors in due order.

Each row had a monitor who checked any vacant seats and reported to whatever powers-that-be . . . . The only acceptable excuses for absence were illness, absence from the city, battle, murder, or sudden death.

GOLDIE CAPERS SMITH

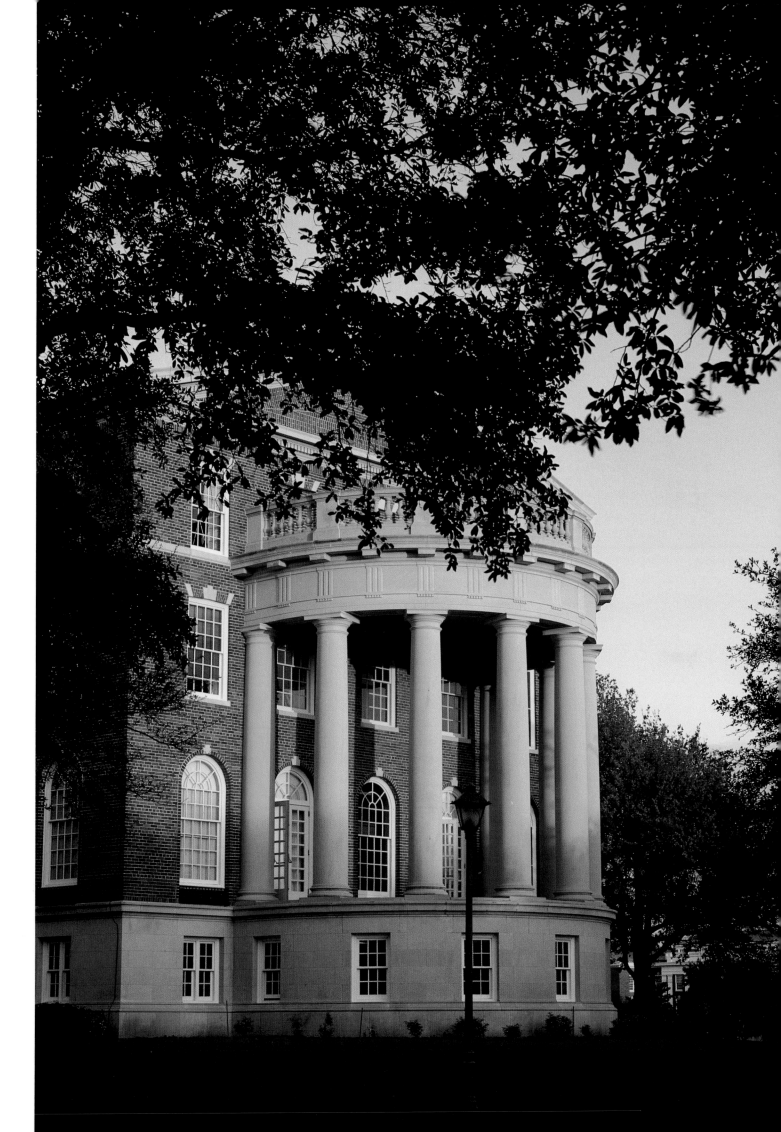

The campus was mostly just a field of wild flowers, and way down at the end of the campus . . . was a little wooden building that was the Highland Park Methodist Church and the few trees in there now were then numerous. There was a creek through there when I came to school. The creek would sometimes flood and be all across the streetcar track, for instance. It was little, but in time of rain it would just flood out onto the street. . . .

Miss Mary McCord rehearsed knowing that they were going to produce the play out of doors, and because of that the first play was *As You Like It*, in which most of the play is in the forest of Arden. . . . The play was reviewed by the *Dallas Morning News* and the article said that there were a thousand people in the audience. They sat on blankets on the wild grass there; they sat on top of cars.

EDYTH M. RENSHAW

Another event I remember, which you may want to forget. A bunch of the boys were whooping it up one night and lit on a creative idea. One was dressed as a demi-rep in clothes borrowed from the girls' dorm. Then a fellow with a mind like a serpent looked up a freshman in the boys' dorm, letting him know, as a friend, that excitement was available in the Forest of Arden. He took the whole hook, line, and sinker, and made his trembling way to the trysting place, now deserted but for the bogus demi-rep. At the precise moment, the conspirators came out yelling, yaa, yaa, from behind trees and bushes. I'm sure he has forgotten it by now, and is probably a loving husband and doting grandfather.

GEORGE MILES GIBSON

When the United States entered the First World War in the Spring of 1917, I had conferences in all my free moments with young men who were entering into the service of their country. To this day I can remember many of those conversations and I can see the faces of those boys as they talked to me. I recall one student who was planning to enter the ministry and had just been licensed to preach. I asked him whether he intended to go into the chaplaincy or the officers' training school. His reply was, "I am so deeply concerned about the situation that I am planning to volunteer as a private in the infantry." That he did, and on the morning of November 11, 1918, just an hour before the armistice, he was killed.

IVAN LEE HOLT

Military drills continued on campus. Coeds learned to knit and wrap bandages at weekly meetings with the Red Cross. By the time the Armistice was signed on November 11, 1918, more than 500 boys were in the "war to end wars."

On Armistice Day, 600 whooping, hollering and yelling eds and coeds squeezed themselves into three trolleys and headed to town for a victory celebration. They formed a parade at Austin Street and marched down Elm singing "Hail, Hail, the Gang's All Here" and "It's Over Over There," and occasionally paused for a few SMU songs and yells in which the townfolk lustily joined.

THE MUSTANG, OCTOBER 1964

Of course, there were no paved streets. Hillcrest was not paved. University, McFarlin—these were dirt roads. There was a so-called dinkey streetcar which ran from Knox Street to Dallas Hall on Hillcrest. One walked on two board planks up to Dallas Hall and from there down to the Woman's Building. When one was unfortunate enough to slip on the planks or when the rain was so severe that the boards wobbled, one slipped into rich, black mud. It was several years before the streetcar owners decided to build a small shed at the end of the line so that those of us who got off in a pouring-down rain or who came to wait for the dinkey could at least be sheltered somewhat from the storms.

ELISE HAY (MRS. J. ROSCOE) GOLDEN

A student's car parked on the campus in those days would have drawn a crowd as curious as would a visitor from the moon today. Only a few of the faculty members drove cars to class. Few families owned a car; if they did, it was not for the use of the younger members of the family. A majority of the students lived in Dallas, and our connecting link between the hill and the city was a small trolley car whose track began at Abbott and Euclid, where we transferred to it, and ended at Hillcrest and University Boulevard, amid the Indian blankets.

One other means of locomotion helped a few of us who lived not too far away—the bicycle. Among the bicycle riders was Dr. John S. McIntosh, Head of Latin and Greek, who rode his bicycle for years after the population explosion of cars on the campus. Books in a basket, tweed cap from Scotland on his head, mustache blowing in the breeze, and cheeks pink from the hillside climb, he rolled up to Dallas Hall, the picture of the benevolent Centaur welded to a bike.

GOLDIE CAPERS SMITH

Looking back, I can recall only one serious problem that confronted the Senior Class of 1920 the semester I served as its president. The issue was whether the men of the class should bring their dates to the senior banquet in private automobiles, or as a group by trolley. Transportation by car won out. Student life was thus relatively placid.

S. D. MYRES, JR.

I want to honor Dr. Horace Bishop, a Methodist minister, who had no money to give but whose advice and support were invaluable. He was the first chairman of the Board of Trustees, and for his wise leadership, the broad approach to the University and Dallas Hall was named for him—Bishop Boulevard.

MARGARET HYER THOMAS

One summer our father [Prof. Alvin D. Schuessler] took a sabbatical from the University and went to the University of Heidelberg to study. During that time he traveled in Europe and was taken by the gardens in Versailles. He drew little plans from the gardens that he saw in Europe, and brought them back, and that was what inspired him. . . . Of course, they didn't have money to do things, so he decided, well, maybe each senior class could leave a gift. So he started with each class and they would give different things. . . . I think his proudest moment was when all the trees on Bishop Boulevard were planted. He felt like that was going to be a real contribution to the University in years to come. They were small in the beginning, but they were still beautiful.

ERLINE SCHUESSLER TOMLIN

What few trees there are on the campus have been set there by loving hands or else by those unending ceremonies which have come to be a joke and a tradition—like the "spoonholder" [a bench used for spooning] and the concrete pillars *my* class left the university. But the landscape artist has done his bit competently and the campus now looks almost like any dear old alma mater.

CHARLES W. FERGUSON

Implicit in our work was the commitment to assist in building a university of stature and strength. Yet few of us realized at the time that this purpose would be achieved within three brief decades and that most of us would live to see our hopes doubly fulfilled. Today, as we see SMU standing majestically on the hill, we who were active during the 1920's and 1930's—the formative years—are proud to have contributed our part to this great achievement. This satisfaction is in many ways a reward nonpareil.

S. D. MYRES, JR.

I served on the Hilltop many years while Willis Tate was president. That SMU association, with all of its intricacies in student activities as well as faculty and curriculum and the individual schools, was an education in itself and there is no doubt about that. That relationship with SMU has greatly influenced my life in lots of ways other than just in higher education. . . .

WILLIAM P. CLEMENTS, JR.

Life in the Woman's Building was guided by Mrs. R. S. Hyer, who was a highly cultured lady of the old southern school. She was a member of the Dallas Shakespeare Club and added scholarship to our lives, as well as grace and dignity. Her demeanor demanded ladylike behavior; there was no other kind. I remember Dr. and Mrs. Hyer best from the dining room, which was in the basement. There was a family table for the Hyers and also a faculty table; the rest of us sat at assigned tables. We filed down the steps and remained standing until Dr. Hyer said grace. On one occasion I remember the ritual was broken when Mrs. Harold Hart Todd, a delightful piano teacher who spoke with an accent, slipped on the top step and bumped sitting upright with feet forward to the floor and exclaimed loudly, "I t'ink I say damn." Even the Hyers were amused.

Fortunately there were no problems of smoking, drinking, panty raids, and the like; they did not exist; if they had we probably would have resorted to the pillory. Our penalties were graduated: restriction to the campus for a short time if we were caught chewing gum in public. The girl who rode in a "horseless carriage" on a Sunday was campused for a half term. The girl who had dinner with a boy in a "BOOTH" at a downtown cafe did not get off the campus until she left for home at the end of the year. . . . On Sunday, if one was popular she was invited to dinner at the boys' dormitory.

President and Mrs. Hyer alone gave permission to leave the campus. Couples in groups of four, never just a pair, on rare occasions got special permission. One of those glorious times . . . we were allowed to go to the city to a show at the old Majestic. We missed the last dinkey and had to walk from Knox Street. We felt delightfully wicked.

FLORA LOWREY

I remember a conversation that a national organizer of one of the leading sororities in the United States had with me. She said, "Our sorority has never entered any school in the first year of its history. We wait to see how the institution develops." However, she organized a chapter of her sorority in the first year of SMU. Several fraternities and sororities were organized in the three years between 1915 and 1918. In that same period we organized a scholarship fraternity, which afterwards became Phi Beta Kappa.

IVAN LEE HOLT

President Hyer kept a spavined mare for some purpose, and she grazed on the green in front of the girls' dorm. Two fraternity brothers, whose names had best be unremembered, planted a stick of dynamite on mid-campus and lit the fuse, then calmly waited on the fraternity-house stoop while the old gray mare grazed her way toward the thin smoke signal. She was almost astride it when the detonation came, rattling the windows of the whole northwest side; and the mare, with tail and mane as straight as a ruler, bee-lined her way toward Mockingbird Lane and has never been seen since.

GEORGE MILES GIBSON

Social life on the campus was pretty well dominated by the sororities and fraternities. Now, when Kappa Alpha got me, they didn't realize what a green person they had on their hands. When the announcement came that we were going to have a spring dance, I was told about that as a pledge, and I said, "Well, I don't dance, because down in Corsicana we sort of frown on that sort of business, you know"; and the initiate said, "Yes, you *do* dance. You just don't know it. You go out and take dancing lessons and show up at the ballroom at the scheduled time." Well, I did, and the boys were pretty nice to me. I was taught how to ask a girl for a dance and if she said yes I would wheel her around a few steps and someone would come and cut in before I could stomp her feet.

CLAUDE ALBRITTON

Perhaps the most singular instance of continued cooperation and loyalty came from our sorority women and their alumnae. In the fall of 1951, we opened at one time eleven expensively built and furnished sorority houses—an event unprecedented in the history of women's fraternities. Sixteen years of planning and working together finally brought the fulfillment so long worked for.

LIDE SPRAGINS

The fountain in front of the University which used to have colored lights and shine at night . . . my daddy [Prof. Alvin D. Schuessler] was instrumental in getting the fountain. He got it from General Electric, and General Electric wanted him to go up in Oklahoma to see this wealthy Indian by the name of Fleet who had one of these fountains in his back-yard. So Daddy went to Oklahoma and saw this fountain, and it was exactly what he wanted, so he put it up in front of Dallas Hall.

WILLARD W. SCHUESSLER

I recall very well the day of the stock market crash in 1929 . . . and from that time on the difference between those who were financially well off and those who were working their way through school, as the majority of us were, was difficult to find, because we were all in the same boat.

SMU as an institution was going through the same financial rigors that individuals were all over the country. . . . I think salaries were cut as much as 50 percent and there were some professors who were probably making very little over one hundred dollars a month at SMU in those days. But here again the University went along more or less normally. We didn't talk about the state of the economy very much. . . . The institution had a very, very profound sense of loyalty that it seemed to inculcate in both its faculty and its student body, and without that I don't think it could have possibly existed.

R. RICHARD RUBOTTOM, JR.

The admission standards in those days were simply a high school diploma plus cash. The cash was very important because the times were times of depression and the school was always on the ragged edge in those days. We always had a number of working students, although the school has been known as something of a society school, but I knew plenty of students who were working their way through.

M. WARD REDUS

Let me tell you about another job that I had that was a little bit unusual. I was a member of the University Park Fire Department for, it must have been two years, maybe three, but the University Park City Council employed three students—here again we were a mixture of athletes and theological students. The two jobs I had were in the tea room and the fire department. We spent our nights at the fire hall and we lived in the dormitory there, along with the regular firemen, and I believe we went on duty at six o'clock in the evening and were off at seven o'clock the next morning. There was a room there where the students could study and we were far enough removed from the domino games that went on all of the time—as a matter of fact, sometimes we participated in the games when we were fairly caught up with our studies.

The major fire we had during the time I was there was the old chemistry shack. . . . We lost the fire. We battled for several hours but, of course, the fumes that came out of those chemicals were terrible. We worked at it valiantly but we lost the chemistry shack. We always say that we never lost a lot . . . .

O. EUGENE SLATER

Scores of letters went to families and friends asking for donations of trees, shrubs, and flowers. At first they were not able to do much about replacing the Johnson grass or getting enough real sidewalks where boards were laid across the mud, and it was several years before the hog lot was gone from its location near the power plant. But that year the sixty or more hogs fed from table scraps returned to the tables as pork or were profitably sold to finance purchases of other food.

WINIFRED T. WEISS AND CHARLES S. PROCTOR

One day when my father [Prof. Alvin D. Schuessler] was down across the campus, he looked at all that Johnson grass and his love for nature and flowers and beauty took over, and he said, "I'd like for this to be a beautiful campus." So he went to the President of the University, Dr. Selecman, but Dr. Selecman said, "Well, we haven't the funds for that sort of thing," and of course, at that time they didn't have sustentation drives and all the different things to raise funds, so he said, "Well, I'll take it upon myself." So my father went to the various nurseries in Dallas and found our wonderful gardener who . . . built the little greenhouse . . . and did a lot of planting in the greenhouse to grow shrubs and flowers for the campus.

You know there were a lot of walks across the campus and those are there because Daddy would sit on the steps of Dallas Hall and watch the students between classes and would watch their paths going to different buildings to class. They always took the short route and so instead of having dirt paths through the grass, he decided he would put sidewalks.

ERLINE SCHUESSLER TOMLIN

Contests held by the student body determined the following names:

The weekly newspaper, first known as the *SMU Times*, was renamed *The Campus*. [It became *The Daily Campus* in August 1969.]

*Rotunda*, chosen as the name for the yearbook, was suggested by three different students.

During the second year the name *Mustang* was selected for the athletic team, which previously had had no specific designation.

DOROTHY AMANN

This leads me to the manner in which the *Rotunda* editor was chosen. The fall of the year 1918-19 found most of the boys of the senior class gone from the campus to the Army, Navy, Air Force, and Marines. There was no senior boy left who cared to become editor of the *Rotunda*, and a year without a yearbook was unthinkable. The editorship was elective: the choice must be between a junior boy and a senior girl. I was the senior girl.

GOLDIE CAPERS SMITH

You haven't heard of the *Dinkey?* This is the student publication named for the bouncing little streetcar that once ran from Knox Street out to the University. This publication appeared each year on April First, April Fool's Day, between 1916 and 1929. It was often printed in red or green ink. This sheet offered the opportunity for students to lampoon faculty, administration, and some fellow students. Editors were frequently subject to disciplinary action, so not all articles were signed. The bound volumes in Fondren Library make interesting reading for succeeding generations of students.

LOIS BAILEY

I can't help thinking of my own sympathies then and later with Mr. [John] McGinnis and Mr. [Henry Nash] Smith who were trying to put out a magazine with almost no money. I think I, the part-time typist, was the only paid employee, so that the only reason that the SMU Press was any particular expense at all, except for printing costs for a book manuscript, was the fact that I was on the payroll. The *Southwest Review* was such a struggling little publication that I never pick it up without feeling and admiration. A number of people made it possible.

THOMAS F. GOSSETT

The band had been made up, in a large measure, of high school students who played in order to get into the football games free. I had a hard time getting SMU students to play. I belonged to the KA fraternity. In the fraternity at that time was one of the finest bass horn players I've ever heard. His friend was the hottest trumpet player we ever had in SMU. They would sit around the piano in the house and our housemother would "chord," and those two brilliant musicians would do "take out" choruses. I begged them, pleaded with them, to play in the band. But they insisted that "we can't play this type of music in a brass band." I propositioned them: "If I can get the 'swing,' will you play?" They said yes, so I went down to the Baker Hotel roof and listened in on the dance orchestra rehearsal. Looking back it all seems very simple now, but until then it had never been tried. I saw that the "swing" is effected by accenting the 2nd and 4th beats of the measure—whereas the band always accented the 1st and 3rd. So I went back to school and worked with each section. There were two or three tunes we happened to use; "Peruna" was one of them. On the day of the first football game . . . on the old field, before Ownby Stadium was built, when the play came over in front of where the band was sitting, we played "Peruna"—swing style—and the football team stopped playing, turned toward the band, and cheered. From then on we had no trouble getting musicians.

V. CYRUS BARCUS

Miss Amann had a great sense of humor, and it became her job, for some reason nobody ever knew, to name the mascot—the little pony—and so she named it Peruna. Well, I don't know whether you know anything about Peruna or not, but Peruna was a patent medicine like Lydia Pinkham—about 95 percent alcohol. And so that is how the mascot of SMU got its name.

ROBERT MAXWELL TRENT

The School of Engineering was started primarily as a result of a project of the Technical Club of Dallas. . . . Not only did they want to start an engineering school, but they wanted it to be a co-op school. . . . In the beginning the co-op program was four weeks long: the students worked four weeks and then were in school four weeks. . . . After the crash of 'twenty-nine and the Depression, then jobs were scarce as hen's teeth. Imagine how hard it was for a co-op director to be out finding jobs. . . . After the war a vast number of our students were GI's, and they were in a hurry to get out. They not only wanted to go full-time but year-round to get their degrees.

JACK W. HARKEY

Mr. W. W. Caruth gave SMU one-half interest in 722 acres of land north of the campus. . . . Every time we sold off a portion of that land why, of course, the deed had to be signed by Mr. Caruth and by the University. So I spent quite a good deal of time running up to the Caruth mansion up there on top of the hill, and Mr. Caruth and I got to be very close friends. I'd go up there and take the documents he needed to sign along with SMU . . . . I'd go up there and I'd get ready to go and he'd say, "Sit down, you don't have to go, just let's sit here and visit awhile." He was a great old soul. Well, I'd stay till I thought he'd got tired and then I took off.

LAYTON BAILEY

In 'forty-six through about 'forty-nine there were an awful lot of veterans coming back, and the University had about 9,000 students. With the buildings and facilities that we had, it was bad. You had an engineering lab that started at seven o'clock in the morning and maybe there would be labs going to ten o'clock that night. Some of the machines never cooled down so that you could take a reading of the ambient resistance . . . . The Superintendent of Buildings and Grounds taught machine shop, and one of the maintenance men taught welding. We would actually run tests on one of the boilers used to heat the University.

JOHN A. SAVAGE

Upon my coming to SMU as Dean of the School of Music in 1949, I found that every nook and corner of McFarlin, from backstage dressing rooms and vestibules to and including restrooms, was used for recitation, study, or practice. This was somewhat overlooked by the many war veterans who were happy to get back into college under any circumstance at that time. Practice in the room adjoining the stage and classes under the stage had to be stopped during any invocation or performance in the auditorium. Such a situation usually brought many calls for cooperation and complaints from students to my office. During cold weather it was cold and during hot weather it was very hot without air-conditioning. Performances during cold weather frequently had to be stopped because of clanking pipes. Dr. Van Katwijk and I had to use the same studio for teaching at considerable inconvenience to both of us. With the coming of the artist teachers, this studio had to be divided, and I had to share again. The practice facilities became more crowded with increasing numbers of students as the reputation of the School of Music grew.

ORVILLE J. BORCHERS

When they started working on the auditorium, they took the beautiful stained glass windows out of it. They had M's in the windows in bright red on a shield located in one panel. At that time I was helping out over in the Registrar's Office, and May Fee who worked there knew what my connection with the auditorium was. She went over and told one of the workmen that I was over there and was a niece of Mr. McFarlin's, and she wanted to get one of those windows for me. I was so surprised when she came in with it, but I took it and had the M and the shield all taken out, leaving the shield framed in the lead in order to preserve it; I have it ready to hang in our home where we are now. I've used it before and I enjoy it just simply because it is from that building.

KATHERINE (MRS. LESTER) JORDAN

IN HONOR OF THE MUSTANGS WHO IN VICTORY OR DEFEAT HAVE BROUGHT CREDIT TO THEIR ALMA MATER.

PLAQUE ON JORDAN C. OWNBY STADIUM

Mr. Reedy asked me to come in June [1915] and get a field and other things ready for a football team. . . . We secured some rusty second-hand two-inch water pipes, and a prospective student and I dug a ditch from where the girls gymnasium now is down through the middle of the field and connected up the water pipe to water the grass that was not yet there.

Then I began sodding the field with Bermuda grass that I dug up along Airline Road and got to the field in a wheelbarrow. The sodding was far from completed when school started, so the school gave a holiday for the boys to continue sodding. It developed that all the upperclassmen became strawbosses and only the freshmen and I worked at it—so there was not much accomplished. The next summer I got it completed by myself. I did the watering of the grass also.

RAY MORRISON

Dr. Roy Blackwell, osteopath, became connected with SMU football as team physician about 1922, with Ray Morrison as head coach. His first notable service was in the role of recruiter, for he gathered up a group of real football players . . . who laid the groundwork for SMU's first championship football team in 1923. Dr. Blackwell soon became Athletic Business Manager but did not stop there. He formed acquaintances with some of the big-name coaches in the country and brought Knute Rockne to SMU to hold one of the first coaching schools in Texas. He had even bigger ideas. He scheduled a game for SMU with the Military Academy at West Point [1928].

JOHN LEE BROOKS

We had the option of wearing long hose or short hose. . . . Our first year . . . it wasn't necessary to wear headgear. . . . The first headgear we had was not hard like it is now, it was soft leather, like a cap, you might say. So it didn't give very good protection, but I don't know of anybody getting conked out from getting hit on the head.

CHARLES H. TRIGG

They said, "Why don't you go out for football and see if you might not earn a scholarship?" I said, "I never had a football uniform on in my life, but if that's what you want me to do, I'll go out for football." So I reported to Coach Jimmy Stewart [1928]. . . . He put me in as guard and I immediately became the doormat for all the Bob Gilberts and the Willis Tates and all of the people who were bigger and more experienced and heavier than I. . . . At the end of the week I went back to see Mr. [Wilton] Daniels and said, "I'm not doing any good at football, and if you would call the coach, he'll verify that. Please help me find a job." He said, "I've got a job for you in the Haskell Theater over in East Dallas."

R. RICHARD RUBOTTOM, JR.

Doak Walker is a natural leader. As a freshman and sophomore he directed predominantly senior teams without any back talk or second-guessing from the older players. Against Arkansas last fall, Coach Matty Bell sent in Ed Green, the Mustangs' ace punter, in a tough fourth-down situation. In the huddle, Walker looked straight at Green and announced, "I'm kicking." He did—a long spiral that rolled deep and put Arkansas on the defensive. After SMU rallied to win, punter Green remarked: "I knew Coach sent me in to kick but when Doak said he was kicking I didn't say anything. Just figured he had a good reason. Maybe he felt a good one coming on."

COLLIER'S, 6 NOVEMBER 1948

All the administrative offices were in that building [Perkins Hall], including the bookstore. . . . I happened to be going out the west door of the building, and there was a fellow standing there, and he said, "Say, can you tell me what happened to that one-story building that used to be around here somewhere?" And I said, "Well, you're in it."

WILLIAM W. WRIGHT

The man who assumes the leadership of an American university in these days must sometimes wonder whether the results of his labors will be worth the continuous struggle, the plain physical exertion which are a necessary part of his office. . . . But surely also he will have moments when the possibilities of this great endeavor will seem to be worth all the cost.

UMPHREY LEE

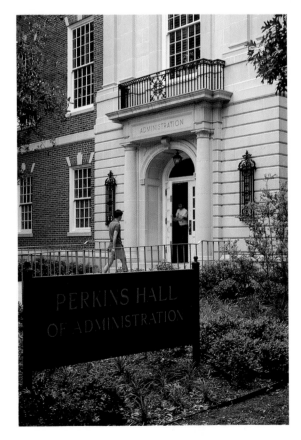

If he [Dr. Robert Stewart Hyer] had a task to perform, the material surroundings made little difference to him. He once said that not even a desk was necessary, that the top of a barrel could hold the papers he needed. When he wasn't teaching or working in the physics laboratory, he did most of his work and writing in what was called the "little workshop." This was a little wooden building right behind Dallas Hall. I believe it was originally the office of the contractor who built Dallas Hall. In this workshop, he worked on his scientific experiments, wrote the Sunday school lessons, outlined his speeches for various occasions, and built his furniture. While I don't think he ever had to resort to a barrel top, I don't remember a desk, just a table or two. But as always, he maintained his dignity under all circumstances, and here in these inartistic surroundings he received many visitors. I have had many ex-students tell me of the personal talks they enjoyed with him in the "little workshop."

RAY HYER BROWN

Most amazing of all, however, is the fact that President Hyer's grand design actually worked—the campus has developed almost exactly as he planned it nearly seventy-five years ago.

LEE MILAZZO

Yes, it is an elephant! The man who provided SMU the money to build Snider Hall back in the twenties was Mr. C. W. Snider of Wichita Falls. He collected elephants as a hobby, and I feel sure that he must have had the elephant put in the gable of Snider Hall to enlarge his collection!

ELIZABETH PERKINS PROTHRO

The girls in Virginia Hall complained repeatedly of the lack of full mirrors. Never could they see the bottom of their skirts and in consequence too frequently suffered the chagrin of petticoats showing and twisted seams in their hose. We had no money, but the need was acute. One day I discovered in a small room across the hall from the infirmary in Virginia Hall a lovely, large mirror, big enough for three full-length mirrors. Immediately, I thought, three floors, three mirrors. . . . I ordered the mirror to be cut at once into three full-length mirrors, framed and hung on each floor of the Hall. Everything went well for a week or two, almost too well, for there was great rejoicing in the Hall. One day, however, Dr. Minnie Maffett discovered that her posture mirror was gone. . . . No college dormitory ever had any more expensive mirrors or even better ones than Virginia.

LIDE SPRAGINS

The administration let the faculty eat in Virginia Hall in those days for twenty-five cents a meal—so even young married couples ate there instead of cooking at home. In the dining room's faculty section, we newcomers got to meet a lot of the faculty, older as well as younger people.

PAUL F. BOLLER, JR.

Our chief duty was the unboxing of books sent in from homes and ministers' studies; the library was started in this manner.

FLORA LOWREY

In Dallas Hall on the first floor, on tables there . . . that was the only library we had; just a whole bunch of books scattered around on these tables and no one to look after them.

JOHN LEE BROOKS

I think Mr. Fondren's son said, "Dad, you build a building these days, if you don't air-condition it, it's out of date when it's opened." So the library is the first building that was air-conditioned.

WILLIAM M. WRIGHT

HEARTY CONGRATULATIONS FIRST IT IS ROSE BOWL AND NOW IT IS A NEW LIBRARY STOP A MAGNANIMOUS DEED BY A FINE GENTLEMAN AND LADY STOP WE ARE THRILLED AND GRATEFUL STOP LET THE GOOD WORK GO ON DON'T STOP.

J. O. HAYMES

The woman who served as librarian and staff member longer than any other, and perhaps knew more students than any other woman on the SMU faculty, was Miss Dorothy Amann. . . . Her keen black eyes did not miss anything that was going on in the library, which at that time occupied the south wing of the first floor of Dallas Hall. Nobody, but nobody had any privileges or felt any rules relaxed within those walls. Not even whispering was allowed. If a voice was heard anywhere, Miss Amann came from the rear of the room, her hiding place, and loudly called for "SILENCE!" Signs were tacked around on pieces of furniture warning users to "BE QUIET!" I am sure that Miss Amann had loads of information at her fingertips, but some timid students, like myself, would rather die than ask for information of Miss Amann. I was as scared as a child of her scolding voice, "Shushu-ing." It is very embarrassing to be singled out as a disturber of the peace.

LILLIAN NORWOOD WALDEN

The library is not the least of your [scientific] equipment. . . . In truth, I feel one cannot say too much for the library and the inquiring mind. . . .

EVERETTE LEE DEGOLYER

Academic libraries always play a deciding factor in the intellectual growth of the student body. As in many young universities, the libraries at SMU developed slowly. When I retired as Librarian of Fondren in July 1969, the SMU Mothers' Club presented the one millionth volume, a first edition of Laurence Sterne's *The Life and Opinions of Tristram Shandy, Gentleman*. In 1983, Bridwell Library added the two millionth. Whereas it took fifty-four years, from 1915 to 1969, to acquire the first million, it took only fourteen years, from 1969 to 1983, to acquire the second million volumes for the combined libraries.

LOIS BAILEY

The late 1940's and 1950's "rained" buildings at SMU . . . . The short-handled shovels tied with red and blue ribbon came out regularly for ground breakings, followed in due time by appropriate ceremonies for cornerstone layings and then dedications with public honors and sincere private expressions of appreciation for generous donors.

WINIFRED T. WEISS AND CHARLES S. PROCTOR

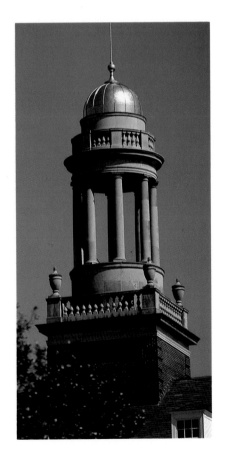

This building for teaching and research in the natural sciences was made possible through the gift of Mrs. Ella Fondren . . . in recognition of that union of science and religion for which the University stands.

BRONZE PLAQUE
FOYER, FONDREN SCIENCE BUILDING

I hope that along with the splendid physical equipment, the proficient faculty, and the increased enrollment, there will always remain something of the idealism that marked the early days of SMU. I hope there will always exist an awareness that education does not consist in turning out thousands of identical machine-made and machine-marked people, but in the development to the highest degree of the potentialities of each individual. This, I believe, the private institution, particularly the church-sponsored school, can accomplish best.

GOLDIE CAPERS SMITH

My chemistry professor, Dr. May Whitsett, repeatedly complained at some point during each of her lectures: "Why don't the research scientists get to work studying the atom, because that is where the energy is present in abundance."

STEPHEN HALCUIT MOORE, JR.

My biology professor [Dr. Frederick N. Duncan] was a gentle person whose whole life was dedicated to his teaching. He had a way of getting his students so fired up about his subject that they continued to work in biology after they had fulfilled the requirements. I even found myself breathlessly counting red-eyed and white-eyed, cross-eyed and cock-eyed *drosophila* in a course in Heredity, and wound up with a biology major as well as one in English, my original choice.

GOLDIE CAPERS SMITH

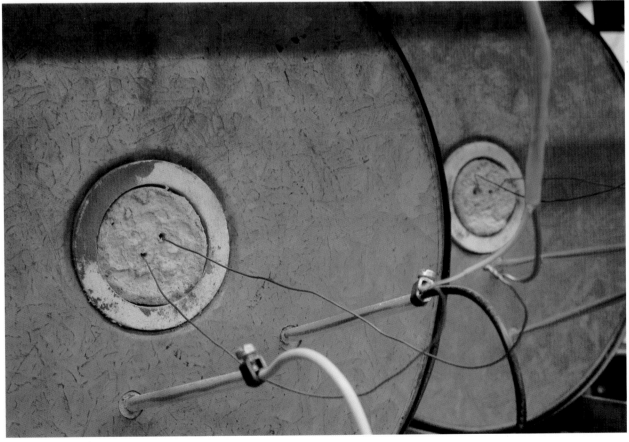

What was it that SMU did for me as a student? Well, it may sound like a cliché, but it's absolutely true: I was a relatively green, inexperienced, untraveled, naive youth of sixteen when I came here, and SMU certainly raised my sights far beyond anything that I would have ever seen in Brownwood. It broadened my horizons in terms of interests, and it really opened up the world for me. The world became a challenging, exciting place that stimulated my curiosity. It was beckoning and I pursued it for the next three decades.

R. RICHARD RUBOTTOM, JR.

The dimension of substance begins in the curriculum and is nurtured in the classroom, but it depends ultimately on the dynamic relationship between those who teach and those who learn. This is why we talk so much about the need for good teachers . . . . A good teacher is a special person with a combination of at least three qualities: earnest scholarship, humility in the face of unfolding ideas, and a desire to communicate facts and ideas so that students may better understand man and his place in the universe.

WILLIS M. TATE

I think humor is particularly important in a university. The administrators who sometimes get far away from the classroom and the faculty who sometimes get far away from reality can make for a humorous (if also serious) situation. SMU has had a great tradition in that regard, which has been one thing that has bound me to it through the years. I think of Herbert Gambrell the historian and Sam Geiser the biologist going after each other. Sam Geiser was representing science and Herbert was representing the humanities. Geiser would say, "Herbert exaggerates, he lies." Herbert would say that Geiser was too specialized and unaware of the world beyond the pillbug. Of course they respected each other and had a wonderful rapport. Herbert's favorite story about Sam Geiser was that Sam was pushing a baby buggy and reading a book and nearly bumping into trees, and when Herbert came up behind him to see what he was reading, it was one of Geiser's own books.

MARSHALL N. TERRY

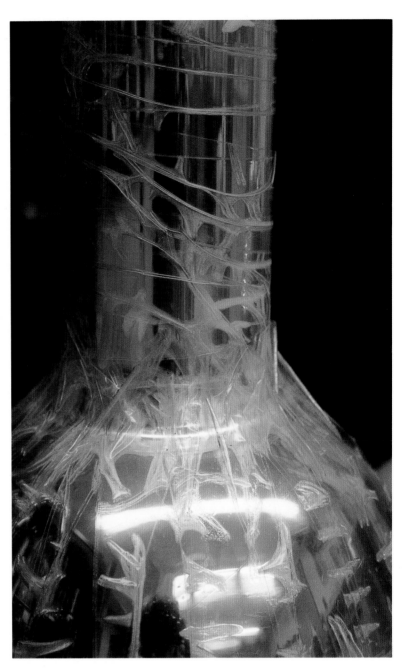

Through vision, courage and love for his fellow man, Umphrey Lee left an enduring spiritual heritage.

LEE TEMPIETTO INSCRIPTION, LAW QUADRANGLE

I remember the first year that the law school opened [1925] we started with about twenty-five students in class. Within a few weeks they had dropped to only twelve students. We had only one professor, W. A. Rhea, who taught us everything, including contracts and criminal law. . . . The whole law school was contained in the last room in the east wing of Dallas Hall. At the time the law library was in one corner of that room.

HUBERT D. WILLS

As the time for school to open approaches, my mind turns to the men who have already graduated from the law school and are out engaged in exchanging large doses of legal information for meal tickets. I should be very glad to hear from you and to know how you are getting along and whether or not you are "sorry you learned it."

You may have noticed from the press that we have ordered several hundred volumes for the library this summer, bringing our total up to about 11,000 volumes. . . .

The prospects for attendance next year [1930] are very satisfactory. The reputation of our school is spreading abroad and I have had a number of inquiries from as far away as Detroit, Chicago, Milwaukee, California, and Florida. I should be glad to have you send me any names you may have of prospective law students.

CHARLES SHIRLEY POTTS

There were not that many places open in the legal profession and certainly after the first few years in the middle of the Depression, we would graduate students here and not a student in the graduating class would necessarily have an offer. There was no such thing as recruitment. Nobody came to the law school to interview people—they got out and hustled and searched for jobs, and if they could get any kind of job, maybe they might get fifty dollars a month. The firms always took the position that they had to educate them in the practice of law, and they weren't worth anything to them—they were a burden to them.

ROY R. RAY

When I came, the whole law library was in just one wing of Dallas Hall. There was a little cage that looked like an old bank cage with a hole for the entrance. A young man was sitting with his feet up in front of the entrance. The library was crowded, jammed up, dark, dreary, and ill-equipped in many ways. I almost turned around and walked out. The young man was working for fifty cents an hour. He was the only one there. There was no card catalog except a little box that looked like it might have been a discarded men's shoe box with some cards handwritten.

The [post-war] students were very serious. They had no place to study. Enrollment was very high. They would check a book out and then go out into their cars to study because there was no place for them to sit down. Even with the poor conditions, the students that were turned out became leading attorneys in Dallas and many big cities of America.

HIBERNIA TURBEVILLE

It is my hope that this building will long stand in tribute to the creation, the preservation, and the enforcement of the laws of God and man.

GEORGE M. UNDERWOOD, JR.

Dean Storey thought that if we had an understanding of each other's legal culture, we might have a better understanding of each other's military and non-military cultures, and maybe we could have peace through law. This was one of his great dreams. He called it "the rule of law." He felt that only by interpersonal contacts could you really have a rule of law where people understood what other people were saying . . . . If we could have lawyers trained in the legal culture, this legal culture would permeate and maybe bring about world peace.

Dean Storey sent my husband [Professor A. J. Thomas] and me down to Central America. We had been planning to drive to Mexico, but he said, "Don't go only to Mexico. You just drive on to Guatemala, Nicaragua, Honduras, and Costa Rica. Buy every law book you can find." He gave us a fund of $500, which was a lot of money in those days. We went as far as Costa Rica, and we came back with the trunk just loaded with up-to-date law books.

ANN VAN WYNEN THOMAS

May I suggest that the size of the donation for these buildings be forgotten? Let's not get excited and emphasize this plant. Rather, let us look into the future and see the many fine young men who come here and finish their training with a deeper consecration, a stronger faith, and a culture which will set them apart for the ministry. When in later years we find these results, we, perhaps, can become a little excited over these gifts. . . . This is your school. We trust that you will uphold it, support it, and love it.

LOIS CRADDOCK PERKINS

Mr. Joe Perkins never made the presentation of any gift without saying, "I have often made the statement that I never had a good intention that my wife did not bear me out 100 percent. Sometimes I suggest a gift; sometimes she finds a cause; but we always work together and get a thrill out of the results."

PAUL E. MARTIN

This institution will develop character in the men and women who are privileged to be a part of it and also through them as they touch countless thousands in the churches where they serve. Eternity alone will reveal the influence of the gift.

PAUL E. MARTIN

Much is expected of you because of who you are and what your university has provided for you. The world desperately needs what you can give. The greatest fulfillment in life comes when *what you have to give so abundantly meets what the world needs so desperately.*

WILLIS M. TATE

Bridwell Library . . . is our collective mind's "yes" to the call to perfection. Within its walls are the materials which in their arrangement and purpose proclaim constantly the profound educational faith that knowledge frees, and that there is built-in in the educative process the only universal self-correcting experience available to mankind. This is our common faith. Otherwise none of us would be here.

I keep wanting to run out of the building—catch the first students and teachers who pass by the shirttails and say, "Come—here, let me show you the basis of what we are—our heritage—our intellectual definitions."

DECHERD TURNER

**I** sincerely believe that the training of the young men of SMU . . . will mean the difference between life and death on the battlefield for many in their future military service. . . . It will be a reminder to young men of future generations that they must keep fit to serve their country and themselves.

UMPHREY LEE

**W**ith approximately thirteen hundred ex-students in the service, SMU also has 77 graduates and exes who have been reported killed in military service of their country. This does not include 27 who have been reported missing or 11 who are known to be prisoners of war in enemy internment camps. . . . Gold stars have been placed on the SMU Service Flag.

THE CAMPUS, 10 NOVEMBER 1944

We had been holding our business administration classes in Dallas Hall. It was the only place where we could hold classes, and all classes were scheduled in the afternoon because the rooms were available only at that time.

In the spring of 'twenty-two, we built a shack out back of Dallas Hall. . . . The shack was built of scrap. The siding was ship lathe . . . . The ceiling in it just went up to the roof. The roof was just rafters. We had classes in it in the summer as well. We stayed there in the shack—they sealed up the ceiling—and they got some fans from the old Capitol Theater, which was being torn down. We stayed there in the shack until 1941.

LAURENCE HOBART FLECK

Mrs. Fincher left personal belongings to be housed in the [Fincher] building. The needlepoint on the dining room chairs she did herself. . . . These rooms were designed to fit two oriental rugs and a long oriental runner. . . . All of the functions like the President's reception were held over here until they completed the student center . . . .

NORA KATHERINE BILTON

What can we do here at SMU that is unique in real estate, because anything that we could do inside the four walls of the classroom could be repeated anywhere else in the United States. The real estate industry in Dallas was the unique thing. . . . There were a large number of very able people . . . in all facets of real estate . . . who were willing to work with me and cooperate with me in building a program. . . . We were trying very hard to show that a business school was appropriate on a university campus and also that businessmen should have a liberal education. This I firmly believe in.

SYDNEY C. REAGAN

It's the students who are here now and those who are going to follow . . . . They're the ones who really inspire us . . . to make SMU still a better university . . . . We will be judged by the quality of graduates in all of SMU's programs.

EDWIN L. COX

Down in the basement on the west side of the rotunda was Mr. Turner's book room. On the one side was the book department; the other side was a soda fountain. Nothing is more appropriate than a soda fountain and a bunch of books, if you can mix them together . . . and some of the good social ties which we had were wandering around, picking up and promoting the gossip which we heard. Some of the biggest issues were batted back and forth around that rotunda and in and out the bookstore and the soda fountain.

W. KENNETH POPE

After the war we got a lot of prefabs from army camps. The student center had been an officers' club, and it was here in the parking lot between Fincher and Caruth. Down where McIntosh Hall is, between here and the stadium, they had trailers. Married students lived in those trailers.

JOHN A. SAVAGE

One veteran remarked, "It's worse than an Army pay line. I swore that when I got out I'd never stand in line again, but look at me now." He was about half a block from the door. At the "co-op" where students congregate for gossip and drinks, the new seating ratio figures about 1,000 for each booth. "From President Lee down," [John M.] Claunch explained, "the university officials hate to say no to any student wishing to attend. But we have had to reject hundreds of applications."

DALLAS MORNING NEWS, 22 SEPTEMBER 1946

Not exactly a "cure-all" for players' "aching backs" but at least a prescribed remedy for SMU's basketball players' feet and legs is the new floor going in at Perkins gym. As planned now the underflooring will be of $2 \times 2$'s criss-crossed above the concrete and under the maple flooring from White gym. The raising of the floor will mean, of course, that the goals will have to be raised. Work began on the project about two weeks ago under the direction of Sid Halliday, Pony grid ex-captain. Workmen on the project are SMU athletes. It is not known when the job will be completed, but the gym will be ready for fall basketball practice.

THE CAMPUS, 31 JULY 1947

We had a gym in which I played basketball. At that time the gym was over by where the old dormitories were burnt down, and I played basketball there, and that court was a lot smaller than the courts are now and we didn't have near the big people that we have now. If we could find somebody six feet tall, why he was a good center. I was a guard and I made one point during the whole season, and each one had a quadrant and the guard couldn't move out of his quadrant. The forwards and the center would move, and I think the game at that time, if you got twelve points, that was a big score in the thirties.

WILLARD W. SCHUESSLER

I went to SMU as an instructor in English, fresh from my undergraduate years at Wellesley, in the fall of 1916, at the ripe age of twenty-one, with no experience whatsoever. I arrived to find myself the only woman on the academic faculties, the only Episcopalian, and one of the very few northerners and/or Republicans in the fold. This was somewhat intimidating, but I had the brashness of youth, and was determined not to be a mouse. In fact, my youth and my sex probably procured more tolerance for me than I deserved.

I lived on Haynie Avenue in a brown bungalow adjacent to Turtle Creek, with the Morrisons (Coach Morrison was the football coach). They were very good to me and allowed me to keep milk in their refrigerator. The milk was furnished by Professor McIntosh of the Latin Department, who lived up the street a bit and kept a cow. And very good milk it was, except when the cow browsed the bois d'arc hedge, with unpalatable results.

My room cost me $4 a week, and two meals a day at the boarding house cost only $5. My salary was only $900 a year and I was sending my brother $10 a month to help him through college.

Melmoth Stokes, a rookie instructor like myself, had a Model T Ford and squired me about a bit, and was a most likable person in his own right. But I did resent his being better paid than I, with the same qualifications—or lack of them—that I had. The group with whom I had the most fun was the knot of confirmed bachelors that ate at my boarding house. I was an intruder into that bachelor society and was treated with standoffish suspicion until they convinced themselves that I was harmless, and then they made a Queen Bee of me, even scandalizing Haynie Avenue one spring evening by coming in a body to the Morrisons' front porch and serenading me loudly with "K-Katie, Beautiful K-Katie." I gave them an apple.

KATHERINE BALDERSTON

**I** can remember Chaplain Claude Evans' first prayer at the opening convocation of the University [1957]. It ended with "Dear Lord, make this a sure-enough university." And we laughed, but it became kind of a byword and a motto. I think it beautifully expresses the blend of ambition and striving to be just that—the provincialism and yet the quality of the faculty that was in the place. . . . Claude never said it again except his last year, and he thanked the Lord for helping us make SMU a sure-enough university. . . . He really did give us a kind of a rallying call.

MARSHALL N. TERRY

The story goes, and I'm sure it's true, that when [Ellis W.] Shuler, an outstanding physiographer, decided he would come to SMU from Harvard after completing his Ph.D., [Harvard Prof. William Morris] Davis said, "What are you going to do for books?" And Shuler shook his head and said, "Well, I guess we'll just have to do the best we can and see if we can acquire library funds." Whereupon Davis said to "show up at my house with a wheelbarrow next Sunday and I'll give you some books." So Shuler did, and put in one of the hardest days of labor that he had in his life, because Davis gave him 1,400 volumes and 10,000 offprints. And that was the nucleus of the geological library here at SMU. Dr. Shuler was himself a collector of books and he added his own to the Davis collection and presented both of them as gifts to the University.

CLAUDE ALBRITTON

The Science Library was a librarian's dream. . . . Of course, everything on the campus had to be Georgian. O'Neil Ford [the architect] threw up his hands in horror at the idea of a Georgian building—but he managed, and the only thing Georgian about it was the arcade around the two sides of the first floor, which he did copy from a building in London. But when he presented the plan to the Board of Trustees, he was a spell-binder—he was Irish and he had Irish lingo—and by the time he got through, the Trustees were sure that that was the most perfect Georgian building ever built anywhere in the world!

We had a wonderful interior decorator . . . who was an SMU alumnus [Wiley Fuqua], and ordinarily we could not have afforded him at all, but he was a friend of the University and a friend of mine and he practically gave us his services. We had a beautiful building. It was written up in all the library publications as an example of what a library really should look like.

ROBERT MAXWELL TRENT

Dr. [Jay B.] Hubble told us that the Greeks called those who wrote verse Makers, so why didn't we call ourselves "The Makers," and we went very happily with that title. These were people who had made good grades in English and who wrote poems either for English class or for the *Campus* . . . . There was stress on honor societies in all departments that I knew about. There was an effort to stimulate, to motivate, and to reward competency or originality if possible. The Makers, with the English Department, brought Vachel Lindsay, Carl Sandburg, Robert Frost, Harriet Monroe to SMU. We as students felt that we brought them. Of course, we couldn't have if it had not been for the faculty.

EDYTH M. RENSHAW

Carl Sandburg has said of "The Makers" group: "I am always free to say wherever I go that your S.M.U. has a youth, flair, verve; I would not be surprised at any sort of work of genius that might issue from your group; the feel is there; it has the rebel yell, the lone wolf howl, and the yellow rose of Texas in it."

SMU ANNUAL CATALOGUE, 1924-25

Miss [Mary] McCord was on the first faculty. Her classes were more like private classes and students had to pay fees. When I came, you still had to pay fees for the courses that had anything to do with literature above the freshman class. It was a frill. It was a little extra rosebud on the cake. Now public speaking classes, you didn't have to pay a fee for. If you wanted to learn argumentation and debate, that was legitimate. Preachers needed that.

EDYTH M. RENSHAW

The building of any university is a race between ideas and real estate; Southern Methodist sought first the kingdom of books . . . and other things are rapidly being added unto her.

CHARLES FERGUSON

The Meadows Museum collection began about twenty-five years ago when my company and the Spanish government were drilling for oil in Spain. I lived at the Ritz Hotel, which was just across the street from the Prado. Every day we would go over to the Prado and walk through and visit the different sections and learn something about the artists and the paintings in the various sections. I became very much interested in Spanish art because this continued for several years. I finally decided I should acquire some . . . . Well, each one of these paintings I had a part in acquiring, and it's like having a family of children. Each and every one has personal attachment and I get a great deal of pride out of having been able to do this and be a part of it.

ALGUR H. MEADOWS

The idea of a Fine Arts Center was born in discussion with Mr. Lawrence Pollock on the beaches of Galveston. . . . The School of Music was housed temporarily in Atkins Hall, where it enjoyed expanded although not model facilities. In the meantime Mr. [Hastings] Harrison obtained a grant for the new music building and the University Study Group authorized a New School of the Arts.

The School of Music was considered an institution to itself—an unnecessary "Conservatory" that had to be tolerated because it was making money to help support the University. . . . After a previous attempt to merge the activities of the Art and Speech departments with the School of Music was resisted, a final change was wrought in the School of the Arts which is a recognition on the part of the administration and some of the classical education board that cultural courses do have educational merit and are a legitimate part of the University.

ORVILLE J. BORCHERS

At that time the offerings were amazingly broad for a school that limited in size. There were very few art courses for freshmen—not much room for them. Those art classes were actually held in the dome . . . on the third floor right around the rotunda railing there . . . . There was an iron stairway that went on up and accessed to the dome, and there was enough space in the four corners up there to have a kind of class . . . . So the old truism about art being in the attic was carried out right there. That lasted two to three years. . . .

JERRY BYWATERS

was told that I should write a letter to Charles Sharp. So I wrote him a letter and asked him for a million dollars. He called me and had me come to his office, and he said, "Before you sit down, I wish you would stand there in front of my desk and let's look at each other. I know your mind is all right, but what on earth possessed you ever to write a letter like that? We have been talking about giving $25,000." I said, "I guess I have overestimated what the Lord has done for you." Later he called me to come to his office. "Now, I want you to stand there again because I want to do something." The project he chose in his wife's honor was the Ruth Collins Sharp Drama Building.

HASTINGS HARRISON

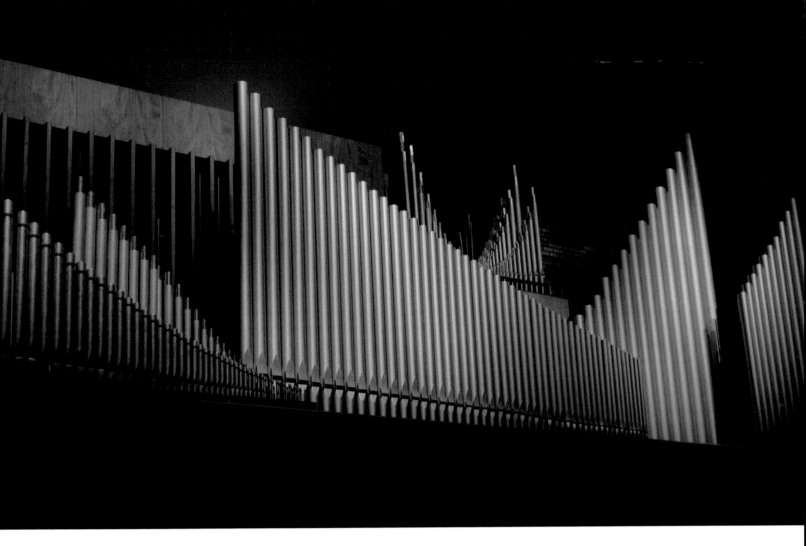

If there is anything more surprising about Southern Methodist than its nationally known aerial attack and its nationally advertised coed, it is the crisp atmosphere of scholarship which pervades the place. . . . There has grown up in the Southwest a genuine movement toward learning and the genius of this movement undoubtedly radiates from Dallas and the University. Bit by bit the school has sensitized a whole territory to culture.

CHARLES FERGUSON

After the war . . . we began to get students who knew specifically what they wanted to do with their time. A lot of men who might not have gone into the arts began to rethink what they wanted to do in life; they had been close to losing their lives and thought again what they wanted to do with them.

JERRY BYWATERS

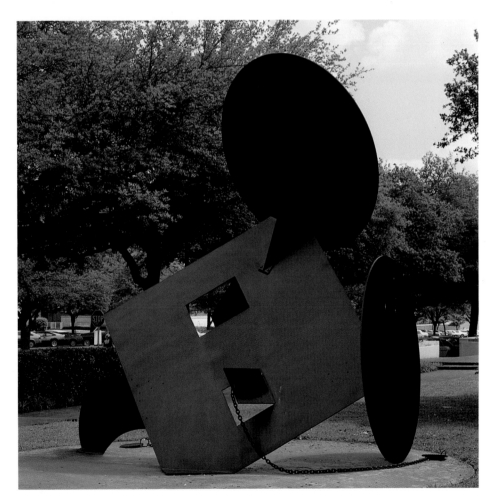

When builders' estimates were received, your building committee saw that available funds would make possible the house, but would not furnish it. At this point, some of the women of the [Alumni] Association were consulted—really a logical move, for isn't home furnishing their favorite indoor sport?

The outcome of the conference? The answer lies not in dollars and cents but in trading stamp books!

No specific goal in number of [stamp] books has been set, for, as in a private home, the furnishings of the alumni house will to some degree reflect the resources of its occupants. It is estimated that the setting will call for an investment of around $15,000 as dollars go, or about 7,500 books. . . . Books will be collected through the alumni clubs in 34 cities or may be brought or mailed direct to the present office of the Alumni Association.

Fun features of the project will be a series of Coke parties similar to the silver tea where the participants will pool their varicolored stamps and finish out incomplete books. It has been suggested that a "licker license" be issued for these affairs.

As the means become available, furniture selections will be made by a committee working with a professional decorator, and the pieces will be ordered through the special order division of the various stamp redemption companies. Emphasis will be placed upon durability as well as beauty.

THE MUSTANG, OCTOBER 1964

I find it difficult even now after all these years to realize that SMU at the time I came was only eleven years old. I thought of it, of course, as a well-established institution, which it was, but I'm sure that the people who had been the founders of SMU and the faculty people—they were conscious of the fact that it was a very, very young institution, just beginning. But to me it seemed that it was well ordered and firmly established and well set in what it was about.

O. EUGENE SLATER

Returning to our triangle [image], may I venture the argument that athletics has a place in a well-balanced education. If the chapel belongs at one angle, and the library at another, the gymnasium also has its essential place.

CHARLES C. SELECMAN

If I were starting over again, I still would be a swimming coach. . . . We take anybody that comes out at the start of the fall program. I believe that is what sport is for, and we are able to do it in ours. . . . We get some terrible rinky-dinks, but I like to think that if it's so good for the good ones, it's good for the rest. I realize a football coach couldn't do this because of the limitations of time and equipment, but fortunately we have the sport and the facilities to do it.

ALFRED R. (RED) BARR

We had a girls' basketball team, some girls with hair flowing free, big hair bows, and middy blouses worn with voluminous bloomers.

FLORA LOWREY

When I arrived on the SMU campus as a freshman, women's basketball was an intercollegiate sport, and big! Dr. J. S. McIntosh was the coach, and the team performed on an outdoors, wooden court . . . .

JOHN LEE BROOKS

Miss Mary McCord had a warm affection for the University and for the students who came under her supervision. I recall that she would have the girls on May Day dance around a Maypole. Edyth Renshaw, who was a protégé of Miss McCord's, said she did it one year because Miss McCord said, "If you'll dance around the Maypole, you won't have to go to gym class this week." "Of course, I chose the Maypole," said Edyth Renshaw.

ELISE HAY (MRS. J. ROSCOE) GOLDEN

Like every other team in SMU this year, the track prospects at the beginning of the season were the most glowing in years. Led by Captain Winston Hooper, SMU's All-American track man, the Mustangs took full advantage of the indoor track under Ownby Stadium, and got an early start in training. . . . Coach [John] Lee Brooks had a nucleus of eight letter-men around which to build the 1927 machine.

ROTUNDA, 1927

I was chairman for tennis of the newly formed Woman's Athletic Council [1916]. To say the courts were not up to average is a modest understatement. Our only activity was having our pictures taken—with racquets held in various incorrect and unauthentic positions. But that met our gym requirements.

FLORA LOWREY

The unoccupied area of the SMU campus early invited the attention of golf enthusiasts in the faculty although weeds and Johnson grass long prevented its use as a golf course.

In the first year of the school, President Hyer and Professor Todd developed a "two-hole course" on the grounds between Atkins Hall and the later Snider Hall. However, the University had little money to spare for the purpose of grass-cutting, so only a minor interest was taken in the scheme by faculty members.

Several years later, in 1920-1921, some of the faculty got together and organized the Hillcrest Club, whose playing grounds would be the greater part of the University campus. By means of dues, set at $12 per annum, the club bought a grass-cutting machine, along with two mules and a hired man to help pull and operate it. With slight effort the persistent Johnson grass was cut and the campus transformed into a tolerable golf course of nine holes.

The club existed until the end of the 1924-1925 school year, when its total material assets, consisting of two mules and a grass-cutter, were inherited by the University.

THE SEMI-WEEKLY CAMPUS, 3 NOVEMBER 1939

If we seek to pick the better prepared students to learn in our classrooms, it is so that they can get on with their work by the side of others who are ready to advance in an atmosphere of concern for the individual student. This must be done with the conviction that quality education is custom-made and not mass-produced.

WILLIS M. TATE

On a recent visit at Commencement I found certain traditions established which we began at the first Commencement in June 1916. At the lunch table one day President Hyer said to me, "I want you as Chaplain to work out the plans for Commencement." When I came to him with the plan, I suggested that we must make use of the cap and gown. The President decided to bring this matter to the attention of the faculty. To my very great surprise the faculty voted against the use of caps and gowns. Since it meant so much to me I can recall almost every detail of the discussion. When the decision was made I told the President that my plan for Commencement was wrecked. With the marvelous tact he possessed, the President asked me to wait until the next faculty meeting. At that meeting he made a statement something like this, "You have voted against the use of caps and gowns. That is your privilege. Those who march in the academic procession must have caps and gowns and the rest of you may sit in the audience." So at the first Commencement we used caps and gowns for the academic procession and have continued to do so ever since.

IVAN LEE HOLT

Our graduation exercises I remember dimly, recalling only endless hours of rehearsals to learn the words and music to a Commencement Ode. We scouted around in the Johnson grass to hunt for wildflowers which we cut and put in buckets and tubs to decorate the stage of the chapel, now Arden Hall. There was a reception in the parlor of the Woman's Building for the graduates, parents, and faculty following the 11 a.m. giving of diplomas.

FLORA LOWREY

And Miss [Mary] McCord at each Commencement would present a play by Shakespeare. I recall that very well because usually she asked me to have one of my students to sing whatever songs Mr. Shakespeare had written in that particular play. One would shower himself with sulphur before the evening of those performances because the folding chairs were set out in the grass and one would be eaten alive with chiggers or redbugs, if not covered with sulphur. So one resorted to the sulphur.

ELISE HAY (MRS. J. ROSCOE) GOLDEN

Mrs. McIntosh never attended Commencement exercises, at which Dr. [John S.] McIntosh was marshal; instead, she stayed home to prepare a buffet luncheon for all comers. The McIntosh table would be crowded with sandwiches and salad and fruit, with a big pitcher of ice-cold milk. The family kept a cow in the backyard, milked by Dr. McIntosh at night and morning. We always thought the rosy cheeks of the whole family might be due to the butter and cream and vast quantities of milk the Jersey produced.

GOLDIE CAPERS SMITH

SMU was founded as a college plus a theology school, and technically that made it a university. Actually it was a college plus one professional school. Then it had a small music school. And then the needs of the city were for a business school, a law school and an engineering school, and SMU added them in response to the need. That was how we were serving society.

MARSHALL N. TERRY

SMU is the finest asset Dallas has. It is basically the heart of Dallas and one of the principal reasons that Dallas is the uniquely superb city it is in which to live and work....

ROBERT H. DEDMAN

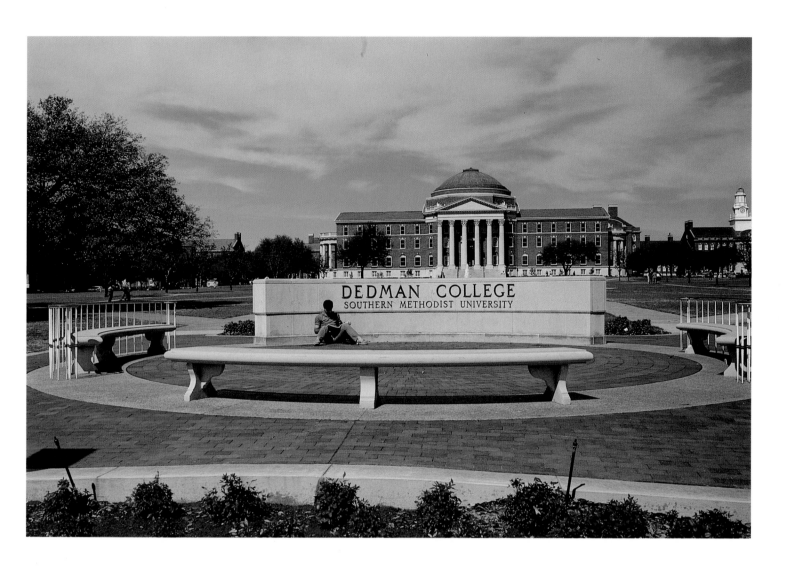

**A** friend once asked President Hyer, "When will the University be completed?" Hyer, ever the visionary, replied, "After the city of Dallas is completed."

LEE MILAZZO

# THE PRESIDENTS OF

# SOUTHERN METHODIST UNIVERSITY

| | | | |
|---|---|---|---|
| Robert Stewart Hyer | 1911-1920 | Willis M. Tate | 1954-1972 |
| Hiram Abiff Boaz | 1920-1922 | Paul Hardin | 1972-1974 |
| James Kilgore (Acting) | 1922-1923 | Willis M. Tate (Acting) | 1974-1975 |
| Charles Claude Selecman | 1923-1938 | James Zumberge | 1975-1980 |
| Eugene Blake Hawk (Acting) | 1938-1939 | James E. Brooks (Acting) | 1980-1981 |
| Umphrey Lee | 1939-1954 | L. Donald Shields | 1981- |

# CHRONOLOGY OF MAJOR SMU BUILDINGS

# AND FACILITIES

KEY: A—ADDITION    N—NAMED    R—RENOVATION    G—GROUND-BREAKING

| | | | |
|---|---|---|---|
| Dallas Hall | 1915; 1971-R | Virginia Hall | 1927; 1963-R |
| Clements Hall | 1915; 1965-R,N | Snider Hall | 1927; 1964-R |
| (previously Woman's Building, 1915-N; Atkins Hall, 1926-N) | | Stanley Patterson Hall | 1928; 1968-R |
| | | Athletic Equipment Building | 1934 |
| Rankin Hall | 1915* | Blanton Student Observatory | 1934 |
| North Hall | 1915* | | |
| South Hall | 1915* | Hoyt Kennemer Fountain | 1935; 1980-N |
| Women's Gymnasium | 1919* | Fondren Library | 1940; 1969-A |
| Fred Florence Hall | 1924; 1951-N; | Joe Perkins Natatorium | 1942; 1957-R |
| (previously Harper and Annie Kirby Hall, 1924-N) | 1968-R | (previously Main Gymnasium) | |
| | | Lettermen's Memorial Dormitory | 1947 |
| McFarlin Memorial Auditorium | 1926; 1961-R | Engineering Laboratory No. 1 | 1947 |
| Jordan C. Ownby Stadium | 1926; 1974-A | Caruth Engineering Building | 1948 |
| Perkins Hall of Administration | 1926; 1938-A,N; 1971-A | Fondren Science Building | 1950 |
| Greenhouse | 1926* | Peyton Hall | 1950 |
| Hyer Hall | 1927; 1943-A; | Robert G. Storey Hall | 1951 |
| | 1969-R | Lawyers Inn | 1951 |

| | | | | |
|---|---|---|---|---|
| Engineering Laboratory No. 2 | 1951 | | Bob Hope Theatre | 1968 |
| A. Frank Smith Hall | 1951 | | Margo Jones Experimental Theatre | 1968 |
| S. B. Perkins Hall | 1951 | | University Galleries (previously Mudge Art Galleries) | 1968 |
| Paul E. Martin Apartments | 1951 | | | |
| Eugene B. Hawk Apartments | 1951 | | | |
| Perkins Chapel | 1951 | | Ruth Collins Sharp Drama Building | 1968 |
| Bridwell Library | 1951; 1973-A | | | |
| Harper and Annie Kirby Hall | 1951 | | Kay Kimbell Garden | 1970 |
| Faculty Club (previously Delta Zeta Sorority, 1951-N) | 1951; 1974-N | | R. L. Thornton Alumni Center | 1967 |
| | | | N. L. Heroy Science Hall | 1969 |
| Selecman Hall | 1954 | | Underwood Law Library | 1971 |
| Joseph Wylie Fincher Memorial Building | 1954 | | Dawson Service Center (previously Central Services Building) | 1971; 1979-N |
| Umphrey Lee Student Center | 1955; 1964-A | | | |
| Boaz Hall | 1956 | | A. R. Barr Pool | 1972 |
| Moody Coliseum | 1956; 1965-N | | Fort Burgwin (New Mexico) Research Center | 1974 |
| Shuttles Hall | 1957 | | | |
| W. D. Bradfield Memorial Computing Center | 1957; 1962-A | | Greenhouse | 1975 |
| | | | Dedman Center for Lifetime Sports | 1976 |
| Engineering Laboratory No. 3 | 1958 | | | |
| | | | Haggar Tennis Stadium | 1978 |
| Umphrey Lee Tempietto | 1959 | | Morrison-Bell Track | 1978 |
| McElvaney Hall | 1959 | | Parking Garage | 1985-G |
| Moore Hall | 1959 | | Maguire Building | 1985-G |
| Mary Hay Hall | 1959 | | Trammell Crow Building | 1985-G |
| Memorial Health Center | 1960 | | Hughes-Trigg Student Center | 1986-G |
| Science Information Center | 1961 | | | |
| McIntosh Hall | 1964 | | | |
| Morrison Hall | 1964 | | | |
| Cockrell Hall | 1964 | | | |
| McGinnis Hall | 1964 | | | |
| Owen Arts Center | 1965 | | | |
| Caruth Auditorium | 1965 | | | |
| Forbes Music Building | 1965 | | | |
| Meadows Museum | 1965 | | | |
| Meadows Sculpture Court and Garden | 1965 | | | |
| Pollock Art Galleries | 1965 | | | |
| Harrison Building | 1967 | | | |

\* Building no longer exists

Note: Original date represents year of completion *or* dedication.

# INDEX OF INTERVIEWEES AND SOURCES

The information and dates provided below pertain *only* to an individual's affiliation with SMU. Class years were gathered from the SMU Alumni Directory (Dallas: SMU Alumni Association, 1985). Faculty, staff, and administrative dates and information were derived from SMU's official annual catalogues, from *Southern Methodist University: Founding and Early Years*, by Mary Martha Hosford Thomas, SMU Class of 1948 (Dallas: SMU Press, 1974), and from the notes of Dorothy Haralson, University Secretary.

SMU Archives; page *54*.

Brown, Ray Hyer
  *Robert Stewart Hyer: The Man I Knew* (Salado, Texas: Anson Jones Press, 1957), p. 141; pages *12, 50*.

Burns, Aubrey  *SMU Class of 1926*.
  Author of "Dallas Hall," *Rotunda, 1923*; page *25*.

Bywaters, Jerry  *SMU Class of 1927*.
  *1936-71*.
  *Professor of Art*.
  Interview with Lee Milazzo, 19 September 1973, SMU Archives; pages *106, 112*.

Clements, William P., Jr.  *SMU Class of 1939*.
  *1963-73; 1977-79; 1983- *.
  *Board of Trustees, Board of Governors*.
  "A Mustang in the Mansion: Governor William P. Clements, Jr.," Interview with Frank Ivey, *The Mustang* (Winter 1979), p. 3; page *24*.

Cox, Edwin L.  *SMU Class of 1942*.
  *1966- *.
  *Board of Trustees, Board of Governors*.
  As quoted in "Our Quiet Man at the Top," *The Mustang* (Summer 1981), p. 20; page *88*.

Dedman, Robert H.  *SMU Law Class of 1953 (LL.M.)*.
  *1976- *.
  *Board of Trustees, Board of Governors*.
  "Why: The Dedman Gift to Southern Methodist University," 8 May 1981, SMU Archives; page *136*.

DeGolyer, Everette Lee
  "Severinus Brought Up To Date," in *Mr. De, A Biography of Everette Lee DeGolyer*, by Lon Tinkle (Boston: Little, Brown & Co., 1970), p. 235; page *56*.

Ferguson, Charles W.  *SMU Class of 1923*.
  *1973-80*.
  *Board of Trustees*.
  Letter to Herbert Gambrell, 24 July 1961, Fondren Library (Cage), SMU; pages *22, 102, 110*.

Fleck, Laurence Hobart
  *1921-63*.
  *Professor of Accounting, Comptroller, Dean of School of Business Administration*.
  Interview, 9 February 1978, SMU Archives; page *88*.

Gibson, George Miles  *SMU Class of 1917*.
  Letter to Herbert Gambrell, 4 December 1964, SMU Archives; pages *14, 28*.

Golden, Elise Hay (Mrs. J. Roscoe)
  *1919-57*.

*Associate Professor of Voice*.
  Interview with Eva B Slater, 24 September 1984, SMU Archives; pages *18, 120, 132*.

Gossett, Thomas F.  *SMU Class of 1948 (M.A.)*.
  *1947-48*.
  *Instructor of English*.
  Interview with Dorothy Murphy, 11 November 1985, SMU Archives; page *36*.

Harkey, Jack W.  *SMU Class of 1944*.
  *1953- *.
  *Professor of Mechanical Engineering*.
  Interview with David Schulz, October 1985, SMU University Relations Files; page *40*.

Harrison, Hastings
  *1959-75*.
  *Senior Consultant to the President*.
  Interview with Bonnie Hillerbrand, 10 June 1983, SMU Archives; page *108*.

Haymes, Reverend Joseph O.  *SMU Class of 1923*.
  *1933-60*.
  *Board of Trustees*.
  Telegram to Dr. Charles C. Selecman, 3 December 1935, SMU Archives; page *54*.

Holt, Bishop Ivan Lee
  *1915-56*.
  *Professor of Hebrew and Old Testament, Chaplain, Board of Trustees*.
  "Early Years at SMU," n.d., SMU Archives; pages *v, 16, 28, 130*.

Hosford, Hemphill  *SMU Class of 1919*.
  *1919-29, 1946-62*.
  *Professor of Mathematics, Dean of University, Dean of Faculty of College of Arts and Sciences, Academic Vice President, Vice President and Provost*.
  "The First Week of Southern Methodist University," n.d., SMU Archives; page *10*.

Jordan, Catherine (Mrs. Lester)
  Interview with Dorothy Murphy, 25 October 1985, SMU Archives; page *42*.

Lee, Umphrey  *SMU Class of 1916 (M.A.)*.
  *1927-33, 1939-58*.
  *Professor of Homiletics, President, Chancellor*.
  "Dedication of the Joe Perkins Gymnasium at SMU," *The Southwestern Advocate* (2 October 1942), p. 5; page *86*.
  Speech presented at the 1948 presidential inauguration of Drew University's President Fred Garrison Holloway; cited in *SMU News-Digest* (May/June 1954), p. 3; page *48*.

Lowrey, Flora  *SMU Class of 1916*.
  Untitled manuscript, n.d., SMU Archives; pages

Selecman, Bishop Charles C.
*1921-38.*
*Board of Governors, President.*
Dedication of the Joe Perkins Gymnasium, 2 October 1942, SMU Archives; page *116*.
Slater, Eva B *SMU Class of 1926.*
Interview with Judy Mohraz, 28 January 1986, SMU Archives; pages *xviii-xxiii*.
Slater, Bishop O. Eugene *SMU Class of 1930; B.D., 1932.*
*1960-77.*
*Board of Trustees, Bishop in Residence.*
Interview with Toni Terry, 24 March 1984, SMU Archives; pages *32, 114.*
Smith, Goldie Capers *SMU Class of 1919.*
"A Part of All That I Have Met," n.d., SMU Archives; pages *6, 12, 20, 36, 62, 64, 134.*
Spragins, Lide *SMU Class of 1917.*
*1937-57.*
*Associate Professor of English, Dean of Women.*
Letter to Herbert Gambrell, 4 June 1965, SMU Archives; pages *28, 52.*
Tate, Willis M. *SMU Class of 1932; M.A., 1935.*
*1945-72.*
*Professor of Sociology, President, Chancellor.*
"The Fourth Dimension of Christian Education," in *Willis M. Tate: Views and Interviews,* ed. Johnnie Marie Grimes (Dallas: SMU Press, 1978), pp. 6, 7, 20; pages *68, 82, 128.*
Interview with Eva B Slater, 18 June 1985, SMU Archives; page *xiv.*
Terry, Marshall N. *SMU Class of 1953; M.A., 1954.*
*1954-.*
*Professor of English.*
Interview with Bonnie Hillerbrand, 28 December 1985, SMU Archives; pages *xviii, 68, 96, 136.*
Thomas, Ann Van Wynen *SMU Law Class of 1952 (LL.M.).*
*1965-85.*
*Professor of Political Science.*
Interview with Donna Salacuse, 15 March 1986, SMU Archives; page *76.*
Thomas, Margaret Hyer *SMU Class of 1923.*
"Recollections of SMU," April 1982, SMU Archives; pages *3, 6, 22.*
Tomlin, Erline Schuessler *SMU Class of 1935.*
Interview with Billy Ruth Rubottom, 21 March 1984, SMU Archives; pages *22, 34.*
Trent, Robert Maxwell
*1949-71.*

*Director of Libraries.*
Interview with Bonnie Hillerbrand, 5 March 1984, SMU Archives; pages *38, 98.*
Trigg, Charles H. *SMU Class of 1929.*
*1935-42, 1946-47.*
*Professor of Physical Education, Coach.*
Interview with Bonnie Hillerbrand, 9 May 1985, SMU Archives; page *46.*
Turbeville, Hibernia
*1947-74.*
*Law Librarian.*
Interview with Donna Salacuse, 15 March 1986, SMU Archives; page *74.*
Turner, Decherd
*1950-80.*
*Professor of Bibliography, Bridwell Librarian.*
Address given at Perkins Honors' Day, 20 March 1968, Bridwell Library, SMU; page *84* (top).
Letter to Clifford [Tinsley] and Herbert [Story], 26 April 1968, Bridwell Library, SMU; page *84* (bottom).
Underwood, George M., Jr. *SMU Class of 1941.*
*1968-.*
*Board of Trustees, Board of Governors.*
"Dedication of the Underwood Law Library," *The Brief* (Fall 1971), p. 1; page *74.*
Walden, Lillian Norwood *SMU Class of 1921.*
Letter to Herbert Gambrell, 6 February 1965, SMU Archives; page *56.*
Weiss, Winifred T.
*Umphrey Lee: A Biography,* with Charles S. Proctor (Nashville and New York: Abingdon Press, 1971), pp. 32, 162; pages *34, 58.*
White, James F.
*1961-83.*
*Associate Professor of Worship.*
*Architecture at SMU: 50 Years and Buildings* (Dallas: SMU Press, 1966), p. 3; page *3.*
Wills, Hubert D. *SMU Law Class of 1928 (LL.B.).*
Interview with Donna Salacuse, 17 February 1986, SMU Archives; page *70.*
Interview with Roddy Wolper, 26 August 1985, SMU University Relations Files; page *70.*
Wright, William M. *SMU Class of 1936.*
*1934-85.*
*University Financial Officer.*
Interview with Dorothy Murphy, 13 June 1985, SMU Archives; pages *48, 54.*

# PHOTOGRAPHIC CREDITS

All black-and-white photographs in the Introduction are courtesy of the SMU Archives.

NOTE: Initials after each photograph listed below indicate the photographer.

| | | | | |
|---|---|---|---|---|
| JC | Janet Coleman | WS | William Stallcup |
| NC | Nan Coulter | PT | Paul Talley |
| LE | Laury Egan | WW | Winky Waugh |
| EP | Elizabeth Prothro | SMU | Media Center, Sports Information Office, University Relations |
| MS | Mark Smith | | |